The Inner Athlete

The Inner Athlete: Mind Plus Muscle for Winning

Robert M. Nideffer, Ph.D.

Thomas Y. Crowell Company
New York
Established 1834

Manufactured in the United States of America

Library of Congress Cataloging in Publication Data
Nideffer, Robert M
   The inner athlete.

   1. Sports—Psychological aspects. 2. Physical
education and training—Psychological aspects. I. Title.
GV706.4.N5   796'.01'9   76-8894
ISBN 0-690-00961-5

10   9   8   7   6   5   4   3   2   1

To Rick, who believed he could fly;
to the Swim and Sun divers;
and to Peggy, Bobby, and Jimmy

Contents

Introduction

As I think back on pregame pep talks, I remember hearing my football coach say, "Show me someone with heart and I'll show you a winner." Another favorite saying of his was, "Winning is ten per cent physical and ninety per cent mental." We were always being told about the importance of attitude and mental preparation. Of course if the team lost or performed poorly, we were accused of "choking" or being psyched out. On those rare occasions when the coach felt that I personally had performed well, he attributed it to my being psychologically ready or psyched up. Win, lose, or tie, the difference between my various performances was most often seen as psychological.

As I think back on those times, I also remember feeling frustrated because I couldn't seem to give the coach what he expected of me. I couldn't even understand what he was telling me, and gradually my frustration turned to anger as I realized that the things he said didn't make any sense—he didn't understand what it meant to be up for a game any better than I did. No wonder we didn't communicate!

Looking back at those days from the vantage point of a

psychologist, I now find it remarkable, despite the large number of coaches who attribute so much importance to the psychological aspects of athletic performance, that they most often continue to completely ignore these factors in training. Coaches teach athletes how to punt, pass, and run. Every physical aspect of the sport is emphasized almost to the point of parody. Professional and college athletes may train between three to seven hours a day for as many as six days a week, depending on the sport. They watch videotape replays of both their practice sessions and actual games. They watch game films. When they're not practicing, they're watching someone else perform. Coaches have spring training, daily doubles, pregame strategy sessions, and postgame postmortems. And *all* this training is directed toward that ten per cent physical readiness my old coach liked to talk about. As for the ninety per cent mental stuff, the athlete is simply sent home with the same old tired instructions, "Be hungry," "Psych yourself up," or the all-purpose "Get ready!" It would be funny if it weren't so sad.

Naturally enough there's a variety of reasons for the failure of many coaches to systematically teach athletes about the importance of their mental and psychological states and attitudes. For starters, often the coach doesn't really understand the importance of these elements, despite all the lip service he may give to being psyched up and to the avoidance of "choking." In point of fact these terms convey very little meaning because they are vague and imprecise. What the coach is often saying is, play as well and as hard as you can. Still, what does this mean to the individual athlete? People aren't machines and they're not always predictable. How does the athlete psych himself up?

Once the game is over, how can the athlete tell if he was

mentally ready for the contest? Often it's assumed that if his team won or if he won in individual competition, his winning mental state was self-evident. But that doesn't necessarily follow. Language is used so carelessly that the athlete finds inconsistency in its application to him. What is a winning mental attitude? During the 1975 baseball season, a fight broke out between two of the Oakland A's players in their dugout. Since the team was on its way to another division championship, the manager and others saw it as evidence of the team's finely honed competitiveness and high spirits. However, if the team had been losing, the fight would have been interpreted as a sign of team dissension or a lack of unity. No wonder athletes become confused both by the instructions they receive with regard to preparing themselves for competition and by the official response to their performances. If we believe the TV sports announcers, everything is psychological. If your predictions aren't going as expected, the psychological forces must have shifted. This all sounds very intelligent and sophisticated, but it has no rational basis.

The imprecision in language and the lack of definition for terms such as *psyched up* have been paramount factors in preventing athletes from learning how to compete at their best. And there are obvious explanations for this situation, apart from the coaches' reluctance—or inability—to give more than lip service to the need for mental and psychological preparation for athletics. For example, it's a common occurrence to blame a defeat—or to base the other team's victory—on ill-defined psychological factors. It's far easier to do that than to accept responsibility for the outcome. Rather than say, "Boy, I stunk," the coach or athlete says, "My team played okay, but the other guys were really 'up'—they played way over their heads today." This protects the coach's image of his team and the athlete's image of himself. And it also works the other way. "Yeah, I played poorly," explains the athlete, "but it wasn't really *me* out there today." Then you hear all the reasons and rationales for the poor performance. These may range from a bad night's sleep to illness in the family (which can certainly be an honest explanation) to a myriad of outside factors.

Conversely, an athlete, when he attributes a win to psychological factors, may be doing a subtle copout for future performances. By explaining that he was psyched up for a game, the athlete may be preparing himself and others to accept poorer performance at some future time. After all, winning and performing well place considerable pressure on the individual to maintain his high level of performance. Winning becomes expected and often a player can't hold up under the pressures that his success creates. One of the most dramatic examples of this transpires when a widely heralded college football player gets into the pro ranks with record-breaking statistics and reams of newspaper and magazine copy as part of his equipment. Heisman Trophy winners like Terry Baker, Billy Cannon, John Huarte, Pat Sullivan, and Gary Beban are but a few examples of the All-Americans who didn't live up to the potential pro stardom indicated by their college careers. Looking at it another way—and this is a good opportunity to play trivia games—merely consider how many of the Rookie of the Year awards in the various professional sports have been accorded players who didn't come into the pro ranks with all the hoopla and grandiose predictions of glory.

The implication is not that psychological factors are unimportant. Quite the contrary, as I hope this book will demonstrate, but so long as these factors are ill defined, they can be used by individuals not only to avoid accepting responsibility for their performance failures but also to explain away their peak performances. This need to have an easy explanation for everything may very well be a prime reason that psychological terms have not been more clearly defined. If I say to you, "I want you to psych yourself up for this game," I may be providing you with a perfect copout. On the other hand, if I work with you to create a confident and relaxed attitude toward athletics, and teach you how to concentrate, we both know what goals we're working to achieve.

Another important reason that more emphasis has not been placed on the psychological preparation of athletes is the failure of psychological thinking itself to provide a theoretical (conceptual) framework in this field—one that allows us consistently to understand, predict, and control the various mental factors which determine the outcome of competitive situations. Although we are a long way from scaling this plateau of understanding, this book illustrates that a start has been made and we no longer are standing at ground zero.

To the public or to the uninitiated athlete or coach, this whole area may seem more novelty than reality because they have seen only isolated reports in the press of a particular psychological technique, such as hypnosis, transcendental meditation, or mental rehearsal, being used to dramatically improve or impair an athlete's performance. For example, millions of television viewers watched Arthur Ashe appear to meditate during his match with Jimmy Connors. On the other hand, there have certainly been occasions—most of which go unreported—where these same techniques have failed to help the athlete. To cite one example, a few years ago when the Australians were beating the world in swimming, there was a story going around among world class swimmers that the Aussies were being hypnotized and then given a posthypnotic suggestion that they were being chased by sharks. This presumably is what made them swim so fast. One of our own swimmers, a world class backstroker, experimented along these lines, but unfortunately he forgot to turn when he reached the end of the pool because he was too busy escaping from the sharks.

In any case, the apparent inconsistency in successful applications of these various techniques as well as their "pop" appeal have made it difficult for coaches and athletes to place much faith in them. However, I believe that we have appropriate techniques to teach athletes to control mental processes, and these include things like hypnosis and meditation. Past failures are instances of not knowing *when* and to *whom* they best apply. Fortunately we've now reached the point where we can begin to make these discriminations, and that is what this book is all about.

As we've already seen, there exist many misconceptions about the importance of psychological factors in athletic competition. Although they do play a major role in this area of human activity, they scarcely account for "ninety per cent" of performance. Nor are they some kind of magic tool that transforms competent performers into superathletes. Accordingly the first chapter of this book begins to put the respective psychological and physical roles in performance into perspective by examining the martial arts, particularly aikido and karate. The martial arts were chosen for this purpose because, both philosophically and in practice, a major emphasis is placed on integrating mental and physical functioning. By examining the actual performance of beginning practitioners as well as masters of these arts and then by comparing them with the performances of athletes in other sports, we should gain some insights into the potential of each athlete to perform at his optimum level.

Once we understand the relative roles of mental and physical functioning, it becomes easier to discuss the conceptual or theoretical framework needed to tie these aspects of performance together. Chapter 2 introduces some of the psychological variables that must be comprehended if we are to analyze and describe the mental demands of competitive situations. Through the framework that Chapter 2 presents, it becomes possible to recognize and begin to deal with those influences that disturb an individual's ability to perform at his maximal level in competitive situations.

We have learned that the major factor affecting both the mental and physical functioning of athletes, and thus their ability to integrate these functions, is anxiety. Chapters 3 and 4 present several examples of the ways in which anxiety acts to interfere with and, much less frequently, to improve athletic performance. By examining the effects of anxiety and the corresponding arousal that anxiety often leads to, it then becomes possible to define terms such as *psyched up* and *psyched out* in ways that provide both meaning and direction for the individual. And by defining these terms, I am thus able to discuss who should be psyched up or down, under what competitive situations, and by what methods.

Naturally enough, to be able to assist an individual in maximizing his performance, I must be able to assess what his psychological strengths and weaknesses have been in past competitive situations. Chapter 5 describes the various procedures which have been developed for this purpose and provides the reader with a strategy for assessing his own performance along these critical psychological dimensions. The remainder of the book concerns itself with individualized psychological techniques which can be utilized not only to increase or decrease an athlete's level of arousal but also to improve his control over both psychological and physiological processes as well, including the ability to relax. Techniques such as hypnosis, meditation, mental rehearsal, systematic desensitization, and biofeed-back are discussed in detail. Examples of these techniques in use should assist the reader in deciding what techniques to apply to competitive situations. In addition, strategies are presented that can improve each athlete's ability to respond to the needs of other athletes and that can increase a coach's facility in dealing with the individual members of his team. When team members work well together, they are not only a coach's delight but most likely a group of winners.

Chapter One. **Integration of Mind and Body**

Over the centuries, when Orientals discussed the integration of mental and physical functioning, they spoke of being "in harmony" or being "one with nature." Nowadays a coach is talking about the same thing when he instructs his team to put it all together or to function as a unit. To say the very least, these definitions are not very precise.

In the fall of 1975, before quarterback Fran Tarkenton broke the all-time record held by Johnny Unitas for touchdown passes, he responded to an interviewer's question by describing what, in his opinion, integrated performance is all about. "Every coach is looking for the magical, mystical Prince Charming, the quarterback who completes all his passes, calls the right play every time, does everything the coach can draw on a blackboard. Well," Tarkenton then admitted, "that quarterback doesn't exist. People do what their ability allows them to do. The physical part of passing the football is the easy part. With the multiple defenses now, the mind part of being a quarterback becomes the most important. The quarterback has to read those defenses on every play, and he has to believe in his reads. If I can read them correctly, I can achieve success."

Given the unlikelihood of an Oriental master of the martial arts appreciating what Fran Tarkenton has achieved because the Asian is not a football fan, he would still find Fran "in harmony" with his environment—which in Tarkenton's case includes having avoided any serious injury during his career. In any case, the Viking quarterback has more than lived up to his potential and clearly has managed an integration of mental and physical functioning. Using Tarkenton, it's even easy to offer a textbookish definition of this integration of mental and physical functioning: *Functioning is integrated within a particular competitive situation* (playing in the National Football League) *when both mental* (reading the defenses, etc.) *and physical processes* (despite what he says, throwing a terrific pass and running like a halfback and then knowing when to fall down to avoid being injured) *are working together to accomplish a particular goal* (in Tarkenton's case, not breaking records, but winning every game).

Now, without being playful, think for a moment about what this means. Your feelings and thoughts have to be totally oriented toward, and concentrated on, aiding your actual physical performance. This doesn't mean being hung up on winning but rather on playing as well as you can for yourself and your team. It means playing for the joy of the sport. During the winter of 1975–76, for instance, the National Basketball Association's Players Association set up a YMCA program for youngsters where the emphasis was on fair play and team work as well as on self-improvement. We can only hope that this special emphasis on mental attitude—which admittedly is on team play—will get through to the young basketball players. It's about time.

Now, however, getting back to the reality of today, I can

say that while very few coaches or athletes would want to argue with the definition of what it means to function in an integrated manner, very few athletes ever consistently perform in an integrated way. It is rare for even world class athletes to put it all together, and when they do, the results are astounding. Bob Beamon's twenty-nine-foot-long jump in the Mexico City Olympics is an example. Apparently the competitive situation and Beamon's mental and physical abilities were momentarily integrated. (And in an event of this type, the rarified air may have helped.) Since that time, however, Beamon has not jumped within two feet of his record and he is no longer competing. Because he has been unable even to approximate his Olympic performance, it seems safe to infer that the integration, or working together, of mental and physical processes on that occasion was accidental. Put another way, Bob Beamon did not have conscious control over it. If he had been able to control (integrate) his ability, he would still be competing and his brief moment of glory would have been extended. Fortunately for us it is through accidents like Beamon's that we begin to get some idea of an individual's potential. However, we also know that such accidents of integration are infrequent, even for the best athletes. The fact is that in most situations the athlete ends up relying heavily on either physical or mental conditioning—rarely on both. Often this division of effort is related to the age of the competitor, with the young inexperienced athlete relying on strength and the older athlete relying on experience or mental toughness.

For that matter, most of us manage to integrate our mental and physical processes so darned infrequently that when we do, it's like a peak experience—a high. These highs are so rare that most of us chug along unaware that we are running on only half our cylinders. If you think about it, however, I am sure you can remember times when you were playing a game, perhaps basketball, and you seemed to do everything right. When you jumped, you felt as if you were hanging suspended in the air; whatever the angle from which you shot the ball, it went in, and it seemed as if you could run effortlessly.

Yuri Vlasov, the great Russian weight lifter, described this experience most eloquently a few years back in an interview with author Robert Lipsyte, then a sports columnist for the New York *Times*. ¶At the peak of tremendous and victorious effort, while the blood is pounding in your head, all suddenly becomes quiet within you. Everything seems clearer and whiter than ever before, as if great spotlights had been turned on you. At that moment you have the conviction that you contain all the power in the world, that you are capable of everything, that you have wings."¶

Personally, while I have never had this moment of supreme rapture in athletics, I do recall with great pleasure one swim meet I had in college when something comparable happened to me. I was competing on the one-meter board and had to execute a reverse dive with a half-twist. When performing this dive, you approach as if you were doing a regular front dive (swan dive, jackknife, etc.), but as you come up off the board, you lean backwards and look toward the board. At the very top of the dive, you should be in an upside-down swan dive position, with your head and back over the diving board. At that point, if you were to drop straight down, you would hit your head on the board. From this position, your body pivots and you drop one shoulder, twisting so that you end up just missing the board and entering the water headfirst with your back toward the diving board. It's a pretty dive all right, but it can be frightening because the first part of it is blind—that is, you can't see the board or the water—and because after the takeoff, you reverse direction and dive back toward the board.

❡ On this particular occasion, I came up off the board in perfect position. It was as though something had clicked inside me. I knew exactly where my body was relative to the board, even though I couldn't see it. I had perfect control over my body and crystal-clear, complete awareness of what was going on. Time seemed slowed down as if everything were happening in slow motion. I floated up, up, up, and as I reached the very top of the dive, I seemed to hang in the air. I knew that a good portion of my body was over the board and I knew that I would miss hitting the board by about three inches. As I began to drop a shoulder and twist, I heard the screams of the crowd (they thought I was going to hit the board). As I was twisting, my eyes went past the people and I saw very clearly the expression on their faces and the fear in their eyes. I instinctively smiled, feeling such power and control. I exulted in knowing exactly where I was—and in thrilling the crowd. I turned my body and dropped three inches from the board to complete what had to be one of the most perfect dives of my life. ❡

Yet as we all know, these perfect moments occur so seldom that they seem like dreams or distant memories. After such a performance, we often make statements like, "I can't believe the way I played." Even though it *did* happen, we don't quite believe it. Sometimes, as noted earlier, we actually resist believing what our senses or others tell us because that brief glimpse of our ability puts pressure on us to perform at even higher levels. To escape the pressure, we subconsciously deny our own ability and retard our performance despite that fleeting glimpse of what is possible for us to achieve. In the same manner athletes usually fail to realize that they are not functioning in an integrated way because they are quite unaware of the disruptive influence their mental processes can have on performance. Perhaps a simple example of how mental and physical processes can work against each other will illustrate this point.

Almost anyone with a steady hand can light a match, place the burning end inside his mouth, and while still holding the unlighted end, close his mouth over the match without being burned. This simple trick requires no special physical ability but does demand *integrated functioning* because as simple as the physical behavior is to execute, proper performance demands that the person not allow fears of being burned to interfere.

In the early years of life most of us learn that fire burns and we develop a rather healthy fear of it. In the illustration with the match, the fear of being burned causes many people to behave in ways that actually self-fulfill their fears. More specifically, their anxiety results in a reduction in salivation, so their mouths begin to dry. In addition, fear keeps them from closing their mouths completely over the match. If they closed their mouths completely, oxygen would be reduced to the point that the match wouldn't burn their mouths. With their mouths partially open, however, oxygen enters and they do get burned. In this instance, mental factors interfered with performance of a very simple physical feat. Mental and physical functioning were not together. Moreover, once the individual has attempted to do the trick and has been burned, he will be even less likely to succeed the next time. His fear will be intensified, making it even harder for him to clamp his mouth shut.

This trick with the match, while simple, is a potent illustration of what I've been talking about. In 1974 I made an appearance on the *Tonight Show* to talk about the relationship between mental factors and performance. One of the demonstrations that we used on the show involved both myself and Johnny Carson putting lighted matches in our mouths. While this was going on, many miles away a group of girls from a school where I consulted had gotten together to watch me on TV. It was late at night and they were sitting around in their bathrobes. One of them decided to imitate our performance with the match. She was obviously frightened but wanted to show off in front of her friends. As she got the match to her mouth, someone yelled and the girl panicked, screamed, and dropped the lighted match on her very fuzzy bathrobe. The fire was quickly extinguished by the other girls without any injury to this young lady other than to her pride. What she *had* accomplished, although she didn't know it at the time, was to dramatize the relationship of fear to performance.

Each of us can provide additional examples of the failure to function in an integrated fashion. In athletic contests this failure is evidenced by such postgame statements as, "I couldn't concentrate," "I couldn't keep my mind on the game," or "I choked." All of these postmortems refer to mental interferences. It's important to point out, however, that just as mental processes can drastically inhibit physical functioning, physical well-being has a decided effect on mental functioning. For example, take the case of John Riggins, the burly fullback for the New York Jets. Riggins, a fine runner, blocker, and pass receiver for Joe Namath, seemed on his way to a brilliant season in 1973 when he suffered a serious knee injury. Throughout his high school career and then his college days at Kansas, the most serious injury he had ever sustained was a dislocated shoulder. "They just popped it back in," Riggins recalled, but then, for the first time, he realized that despite his impressive physical credentials—six feet two inches tall and a very muscular 230 pounds—he was just as vulnerable as a smaller man. "It was the little kid in me coming out," he later told a reporter. Partly as a result of this injury, Riggins got the reputation of being a very private, even moody individual, but he has learned to live with the possibility of a debilitating injury. Still, that first experience really jolted him. Now, when he's hurt or suffering from an illness (the flu seems to be popular with pro football players), he doesn't let it psych him. "I prefer not to work when I'm hurt," he told a *New York Times* reporter during the 1975 season, when he was suffering from the flu as well as from some muscle aches and pains. "I really need the rest. I've got a very demanding job."

Now there's an athlete who has come to terms with the relationship between his physical functioning and mental state. But most of us haven't made this kind of peace with ourselves—any limitation in our normal physical functioning through an injury or illness more times than not precipitates a mild form of depression in most of us. We become wrapped up in the injury or illness and we fail to use the energy that we do have effectively. Such depression is particularly insidious because our depressive feelings disrupt our ability to concentrate, and this leads to still more failure. The more time we spend feeling depressed, the less productive we are. The more unproductive, the more we have to be depressed about. The result is a tidy little vicious cycle that most of us get caught in at one time or another.

This vicious cycle, however, is not one to be taken lightly. I have talked to a number of orthopedic surgeons involved in sports medicine who find themselves unable to deal with athletes who have completely recovered from their physical injury yet have never recovered their preinjury level of functioning. George Whatmore and Daniel Kohli, in their book *The Physiopathology and Treatment of Functional Disorders*, very dramatically point out how injury and emotional tension can lead to depression and how the depression can then lead to further impairment in physiological and psychological functioning. This same model of tension-impairment-depression-tension can be used to explain the slumps that occur in most sports.

Slumps in baseball are common; even the best hitters experience them occasionally. In the 1975 World Series, the Cincinnati Reds' slugging first baseman, Tony Perez, alarmed the Reds' partisans first by failing to hit well in the playoffs and then going zero for fifteen during the first four games of the series. Perez, the all-time RBI leader for the Reds, handled the slump like the veteran pro he is. "I not pressing. I just in slump," the thirty-three-year-old explained to reporters after the fourth game. "I too old to be pressing. This just one of those things. Tomorrow another day. Got to go day by day, that's all." In the fifth game Perez struck out lustily his first time up, then put the ball out of the park his next two at-bats. "Tomorrow another day," all right.

In Perez' case, it might well have been a case of World Series tension—the Reds had not won a World Series since 1940, and this might very well have been Perez' last chance at playing on a championship team. Most of the time, though, the reason for a batting slump is nothing so dramatic. What usually happens is that some problem concerning family, finances, a girl friend—whatever—results in increasing tension in the neck and shoulder muscles. The tension increase throws off timing and coordination, which of course reduces the likelihood of getting a hit. After going zero for fifteen, the usual hitter starts to worry about his average, and the coach, team, and fans begin asking what's wrong. All this attention sensitizes the athlete to his problem, makes the tension increase even more, and results in further reductions in performance. As he gets even fewer hits, the batter presses more and receives more attention he could do without. The problem escalates further—now he is getting angry at teammates and fans, thereby creating additional tension. His concentration is disturbed, and instead of watching the ball as closely as he should, he finds himself distracted by his concern about going hitless. Finally, he finds himself making changes in his normal grip and batting stance—changes that the coach may actually encourage. All these things act only to prolong the slump and to increase the problem. Given the insidious nature of the problem, it's surprising that more of the slumps which occur do not become permanent.

Unfortunately the failure to function in an integrated way is not limited to those periods when the athlete is injured, ill, or in a slump. Even when an athlete is functioning at his normal level, he is usually functioning at a level far below what he is capable of doing. Though his thoughts and feelings may not be directly antagonistic to performance as in the case of a batting slump, they simply fail to be as consistent or focused as they might be and thus are not conducive to maximal performance.

To be sure, there are logical reasons for the inability of athletes to function in an integrated fashion. The educational process which most of them go through, whether it takes place in the classroom or on the playing field, is not designed to teach them to integrate their functioning. The average coach tries to get his team psyched up for each week's game, gives his players a pep talk before the game, and delivers the appropriate remarks during half time, but as we have seen, the bulk of the athletes' training has to do with physical conditioning and skills. It's an either-or proposition, and the athletes think of it that way. A useful technique like meditation, for example—and I go into this in depth later in the book—would be regarded by uninitiated athletes as a complete avoidance of physical activity, and what's the point? Isn't contemplation of one's navel or one's breathing irrelevant to the demands of day-to-day existence, and particularly to the demands of competitive situations?

Well, this narrow either-or view of what meditation represents merely reflects the Westerner's inability to see these exercises from the framework of the meditator. We look at only the most prominent feature, the quiet contemplation, and we fail to realize that this concentration is much more than simple withdrawal. Of course for the Westerner it's difficult to see how the contemplation affects total (physical as well as mental) functioning, but our scientists have recently begun to examine the physiological changes that occur through meditative exercises and have been able to document their beneficial effects on the individual's ability to relax and conserve energy. Again, it was our inability to see these broader implications of meditation that kept many people from investing a sustained enough involvement in the procedures to derive benefits from them.

Now to the other side of the coin. In the same manner that many people view meditation as a form of isolation and as an avoidance of physical activity, they view athletes as simply physical creatures. These folks openly express their inability to understand how a body builder could devote his entire life to building muscles or how a swimmer like Mark Spitz could work six hours a day to shave a few tenths of a second off his time. Comments about the lack of brain cells in football players are commonplace. Again, this indicates that unlike many of the people actively participating in these events, most of us take a narrow view of what is involved. As with meditation, we fail to see how the swimmer's physical dedication has implications for attitudes and behavioral patterns in other life situations, and we think the physical focus means that he lacks or fails to use mental abilities. Through this narrow view most of us have a tendency to see swimming as physical and meditation as mental and fail to integrate the two, to see that for optimal performance both are involved. More important, our own artificial separation of these processes causes many of us to abandon activity after activity in search of "something more meaningful."

Up to now I've had some fairly harsh things to say about coaches and their failure to understand the importance of integrating physical and mental conditioning, so let me say at this juncture that this isn't true of all coaches. In point of fact this old-fashioned view of athletics as a physical activity with little or no demands for complex mental processes is a sore point with the more enlightened coaches. The modern, really aware coach very quickly recognizes that unless he can challenge the athlete mentally as well as physically, he will just as quickly lose that athlete's interest, respect, and involvement. This sensitivity was driven home to me at a preseason mini-training camp put on by the Buffalo Bills in 1973. I had been asked to talk to the team to give them some ideas about what they could do to get ready mentally for the coming season. When Lou Saban introduced me, he emphasized to the players that I was there because they were thinking men, not animals. He went on to state that mental preparation was important and that it was time that fans and some of the players recognized that there was more between their ears than muscles. Lou Saban is sensitive to his players' mental needs; unfortunately many coaches aren't.

Coaches, even the best of them, have many problem areas with their athletes. For instance, how many times have you found yourself or someone you know bored with an activity after developing a minimal level of skill? In the same way, perhaps one of the greatest challenges in coaching is to be able to sustain an athlete's involvement in an event when he has reached one of those inevitable performance plateaus. At first, learning to swim is new and exciting, but as a plateau is reached in physical development, the excitement and willingness to work begin to disappear. Many people drop out of athletics for this reason. They want more from life—they want a sense of purpose and they need to be able to see their growth. The strict focus on such physical aspects of swimming as time or stroke development makes it difficult to find that sense of purpose once obvious physical development stops. As a result they lose their motivation and drift away from what has become routine practice. All too often they end up repeating a pattern—continually drifting from one sport to another. They never approach their potential in any of the athletic activities they engage in and thus fail to find the self-confidence and feelings of worth they are searching for. From this it follows that the more successful a coach becomes at aiding athletes in integrating mental and physical functioning, the more this motivational problem disappears.

As human beings we tend to develop mental and physical abilities in a serial fashion. For example, a young child just learning to walk enthusiastically concentrates time and attention in the development of this skill. As walking becomes a habit, the child's attention is free to focus on other skills, such as talking. Often the skills which are developed after reaching a plateau form the basis for then redirecting attention to motor development and other basic skills. In sports, once the basic skills are learned, the athlete's attention is free to be directed to the study and observation of the fine points of the game. This mental development—the ability to make fine discriminations, to see what is interfering with continued improvement, to anticipate others' moves, to know where and when to look or react—all this serves to assist the athlete since these accumulated skills are eventually used to improve physical performance and move him off his plateau.

As we build programs designed to train individuals to develop both mental and physical skills within a particular sport, there will be far fewer dropouts. One reason for this is that as new physical plateaus are reached, progress will be measured and observed along mental dimensions that are related to the ultimate goal. In addition, through this integration both coaches and athletes will become aware of a whole new array of psychological influences that have been interfering with their past performance. This awareness will result in a dramatic improvement in performance and in a more rapid development of basic skills. As a result the plateaus which do develop will not last as long.

The Martial Arts

Both the meaning and promise of integrated mental and physical functioning can be seen through an examination of karate and aikido, two of the martial arts. By looking at training procedures and at the feats performed by masters of these arts, the groundwork can be laid for you to gain insight into the strengths and weaknesses of your own functioning in competitive situations—it's no accident that karate and aikido emphasize developing both mind and body.

According to legend, karate had its origins in China through the work of a Buddhist monk, Daruma Taishi, who is reported to have journeyed alone and on foot from India to China. His purpose in making this long and difficult journey was to instruct the Liang-dynasty monarch in the tenets of Buddhism. Upon completion of this task he remained in China to teach Buddhism to the monks living there. Apparently his teaching procedures put such stress upon his students that they became physically incapable of keeping pace with him and some monks actually passed out as a result of the emotional and physical demands of their training. In response, Daruma instituted a program of physical exercise. He explained to them that although the aim of Buddhism was the salvation of the soul, the body and soul were inseparable. In their weakened state they could never perform the ascetic practices necessary in order to attain enlightenment. Thus the exercises were designed to supplement their more spiritually oriented training. These monks eventually became very formidable fighters, and the more modern forms of karate evolved from these original training exercises. The focus upon joint physical and spiritual development remains even today. In this account it's apparent that karate developed as a physical training introduced to improve spiritual development and was the end product of this merging.[1]

The emergence of aikido followed a somewhat different path in that it was the result of a personal revelation. Aikido was founded in Japan around 1925 by a Buddhist named Morihei Uyeshiba, and its development as a discipline apart from many of the other martial arts (jujitsu, judo, kendo, sumo, and karate) followed immediately in the wake of what a psychologist or theologist might call a conversion or revelatory experience. Up to 1925 Master Uyeshiba had devoted his life to the study and enhancement of both his physical and spiritual development. He had spent years studying jujitsu and kendo (a type of sword fighting) as well as studying the tenets of Buddhism. Prior to his conversion experience, however, these pursuits had existed as separate parts of him—he had not yet integrated his by-then considerable mental and physical skills. The conversion experience and the actual integration of mental and physical functioning occurred toward the end of a seven-year period that Uyeshiba had spent in relative isolation and meditation.

As Uyeshiba described it, a golden vapor came out of the ground and the true meaning of nature was made clear to him.[2] He experienced a sense of "oneness with the universe," a deep feeling of belonging to a larger truth. Other individuals have experienced revelations similar to Uyeshiba's, and often these conversions result, as with Uyeshiba, from long periods of isolation or deprivation.[3] In Uyeshiba's case it was this new feeling of being at one with a higher truth which enabled him to respond to his environment in ways that seem remarkable to the rest of us, and later in this chapter we consider just how remarkable his abilities were. The real importance of his experience for us, however, is that it caused him to attempt to communicate some of his understanding and technical skills to others.

To be sure, the ultimate truth for Uyeshiba is not so easily adopted as our own. We do not share his background nor his religious and philosophical tenets, nor his long years of training in the martial arts. I know that as a beginning student of aikido, I found myself turned off and unable to understand many of the spiritual interpretations Uyeshiba gave to his experiences. The effect of my own background was to shield me from some of the valuable things aikido had to offer me quite apart from a religious philosophy. It may be useful, therefore, to examine through a Westerner's eyes some of the classic feats performed by the masters of the martial arts so that we can better understand their implications for us in athletic situations. Then we may better appreciate the seemingly superhuman feats of Uyeshiba and the other masters.

Breaking Boards

Demonstrations of karate and aikido often involve performing such feats as breaking boards or bricks, having an unbendable arm, and keeping two strong men from being able to lift you off the ground. These particular acts can be used to illustrate the relevance of some mental or psychological variables to physical performance. Sophisticated concepts from aikido and karate, such as *ki* (the direction and flow of energy) and *saika-no-itten* (focus on "the one point," the body's center of gravity), can be understood through these demonstrations.

Physically, there really is not a great deal involved in breaking a ten-inch-wide piece of one-by-twelve pine shelving. This is the type of board that is broken in most karate demonstrations, and although the feat looks impressive, many ten-year-olds are capable of duplicating it. The physical preparations for the feat include making sure the board is well dried and has few knots. Having taken this preliminary step, the application of a few technical procedures results in successfully breaking the board.

First, the wood must be braced—held very firmly, preferably by two or more people. These individuals must not move backward or pull away in anticipation of the blow but instead should actually lean in the direction from which the blow is coming. If the wood is allowed to move even slightly, much of the force is taken out of the blow; therefore, the board must be held firmly, with all of the support along the two outside edges. In this way the board forms a bridge with about one inch on either side supporting the remaining ten inches.

In addition to being sure that the board is firmly supported, it's important to make sure that the force of the blow runs parallel to the grain of the wood. Generally, when you hit the board with the fist or with the side of the hand, the grain should be running vertically to the ground. Next be sure that the wood is hit in such a way that the smallest possible surface area of the hand ends up going across the grain. There can be a fairly large part of the hand or foot in contact with the board *if* that part runs parallel to the grain. Hitting with the edge of the hand, for instance, provides a narrow, long surface, much like the cutting edge of an ax. By contrast, trying to break the board with a fist is more difficult because there is more of the hand running across the grain of the wood—the expert, when he hits with his fist, minimizes the surface area by striking the wood with only the first two knuckles of the hand instead of all four knuckles. Finally, for safety's sake, it should be pointed out that when the experts do use the side of the hand, they are hitting on the muscle-covered inside edge of the palm. They are not hitting up on the little finger or on the bone located in the side of the hand.

The factors just mentioned—having the strength of a ten-year-old, stable support for the board, hitting with the grain, and striking with a small area—just about cover the physical requirements involved in breaking a board. Obviously there's more to it than that or else people wouldn't be so impressed when they see it demonstrated.

To the audience the individual putting on the karate or aikido demonstration is viewed as some kind of superman.

He's billed as an expert having special powers that the rest of us are presumed to lack, and when he breaks the board, it's natural to assume that this occurred because of those special powers. In addition this impression is enhanced by the mechanics of the demonstration. The expert wears an outfit that distinguishes him from the rest of humanity— quite often he wears a black belt, a symbol that carries its own aura of power. In effect this badge advertises the person as a "killer," and the audience's perception of this power is further emphasized by the dramatic way in which the expert places the boards prior to breaking them. When the audience sees two or three individuals bracing the board, it assumes that *both* the board and the demonstrator are very strong. It doesn't realize that the addition of men makes it easier to break the board; in fact quite the opposite view is taken. In addition, there is often a loud expulsion of air, a yell, as the expert makes contact with the wood. This also serves to create the illusion that this is a very awesome task. Ultimately even the audience itself acts in ways to increase the illusion.

After the demonstration some of the more adventurous members of the audience may pick up pieces of the broken boards and try to break them. When they fail, this also adds to the aura which surrounds the karate master.

Of course the reason they fail is quite simple. They're working with a piece of wood half the size of the board the expert used, and this means that even if they support the smaller piece properly, a far greater percentage of this piece of wood has something solid behind it. In effect the span of the bridge is much less, and thus the bridge is much stronger. They would have to hit this smaller piece much harder in order to break it. Their attempt is made even more difficult by the fact that they may hit against the grain with the wrong part of the hand. So, just as it's predictable that the karate master will be able to break the board, it's equally predictable that when he's done and the amateurs move in, there will be members of the audience walking around holding their hands in pain. Quite apart from the evidence of one's mortality, this particular demonstration reinforces the seeming evidence of the karate master's extraordinary powers.

Psychologically, however, all that's required to break a board is the maintenance of an attitude that allows the person to hit through the board. He must be able to focus all his attention on a spot a couple of inches behind the board. His task is to drive his hand through the board to that spot. Although the physical demands are really quite minimal, the mental demands make it quite difficult for the average person to prepare himself psychologically to break that board. People almost instinctively pull back when an object is blocking their way. This is true even if the object is no more awesome than a piece of string. Watch a group of competitors at a track meet sometime and see how many of them pull up at the tape marking the finish of the race, sometimes losing rather than driving through it. When the string is a piece of wood and when all the fears associated with hitting that wood are present, it's small wonder that most people fail to follow through. Let me temper this by saying that obviously as the number of boards an individual attempts to break at one time increases, so do the physical and psychological demands. There are limits to what an individual can do mentally and/or physically without actual, extended training.

As we have seen, few athletes even begin to realize the extent to which thoughts directly influence physical abilities nor do they realize the ease with which they are physically and psychologically manipulated by their competitive environments. They get psyched out by their competition in the same way the audience gets psyched out by the karate demonstration. Let's examine, therefore, two procedures that experts in aikido often use to emphasize the necessity of being able to direct and focus attention completely. Both these demonstrations illustrate some of the relationships between thought and movement.

The Unbendable Arm–the Focus of Ki

The first demonstration requires that one person attempt to bend another person's arm. It's performed by having the two individuals face each other. Person A places the back of his right wrist, arm extended and palm up, on person B's left shoulder. Person B then interlocks his fingers over the top of person A's arm and pulls down on the arm at the elbow. With most people it's very easy to bend the arm in this manner, yet with the aikido expert the arm is unbendable. When asked how this is accomplished, the aikido expert attributes his unbendable arm to the flow of *ki,* this being his ability to concentrate and mentally direct the flow of all energy in any direction he chooses. In this instance the energy is directed out through the tips of the fingers on the right hand. This requires concentration rather than strength, and this ability to concentrate distinguishes the expert from other individuals. An analysis of what is actually taking place helps both in understanding *ki* and in showing the importance of mental factors in this demonstration.

When most of us are challenged to keep another person from bending our arm, the first thing we do is tense the muscles in our forearm and biceps. Unfortunately these muscles are antagonistic to keeping the arm straight. In fact they are the very muscles used to bend the arm, and so our natural response to this challenge results in tensing muscles that actually assist the person who is trying to bend the arm. In effect we defeat ourselves.

What the expert in aikido has discovered is that by thinking of extending *ki* out through the fingertips, he automatically relaxes the biceps and flexes the triceps muscles in the back of the arm. These muscles rather than the biceps serve to keep the arm straight. It's easy for you to feel the difference between the two ways of responding. Hold your arm out in front of you, palm up, with a slight bend at the elbow. As you think of extending force out through your fingers, you should feel your elbow extending up in a vertical direction and your fingers extending away from your body. This small difference results in the relaxation and extension which make the arm unbendable.

Once again, as with the board, the simple psychological influence emphasized in the unbendable-arm demonstration has much broader implications for athletic performance. For example, a lineman in football attempting to pass block may drop back and tense his muscles in the same way most people do when challenged. This cocking of the arms to strike out can work against the lineman rather than for him. Movements are slowed down due to the initial antagonistic tension, and the biceps must relax before extension can take place. More importantly though, that tension can actually assist the opposing lineman in driving the pass blocker back into the quarterback. If the incoming lineman hits the defender before he begins his extension, then the defender's own muscle tension helps to drive him back. Bud Winter, the track coach at San Jose State, points out the same problem of tensing antagonistic muscles as it applies to sprinting. He insists that a clenched fist or set jaw is the mark of a loser. His advice to athletes is to run at four-fifths speed instead of all out. He believes that the desire to run all out results in tensing those antagonistic muscles and thus slows the athlete down.

There are many other sports where there is a tendency to tense the muscles in the biceps when getting ready to respond. In most of these cases such tension is antagonistic to what the athlete is trying to accomplish. Examples include boxing or any event requiring extension of the arm, such as the shot put, javelin, throwing a ball, etc. One of the reasons that so few individuals ring the bell on the strength tester at the circus is that they are so worked up about performing in front of their girl friend or an audience that they tense the biceps muscles. This tension keeps them from getting a full extension and from coming down with the sledge hammer as hard as they are capable of doing.

Saika-no-itten—*Focus on "the One Point"*

Another demonstration that the masters of aikido use to illustrate the relationship between thought and movement involves *saika-no-itten*—focusing attention on "the one point." As a student of the art in Japan, I was told that when I could let my mind rest at "the one point" (a spot approximately two inches behind the navel), I would simultaneously be calm and almost immovable. My instructor, to illustrate this point, stood with his feet apart (approximately in line with his shoulders) and with his arms extended down by his sides. He then positioned two of us, one on either side of him, and told us to grab one of his wrists with both of our hands. He then thought *up*—that is, he thought about being lifted, and we found that we could pick him up quite easily. Next he thought *down*, directing his energy down and directing his mind to "rest" on "the one point." On these occasions we found that we were unable to pick him up.

At first I was both mystified and frustrated by all this. I found the idea of letting my mind rest just behind my navel absurd. I very literally translated what he was saying to mean that I should place my brain in my stomach. I knew that this was impossible and so I found myself silently arguing with what he was saying. The argument had to be silent because if I had verbalized it, he would have taught me an object lesson by making me work extra hard or by exerting a little more pressure when he twisted my arm. As a student I was angry with him for telling me stupid things, angry at myself for not telling him what I thought, and the whole time not paying attention to the things the master said that would allow me to understand. Finally, after working through the anger in several months of daily workouts, I began to see and to understand.

The aikido master's demonstration looked very impressive, yet with just a little instruction most of us can duplicate it. In fact, it's not impossible for a woman weighing no more than a hundred pounds to keep two average-sized men from lifting her in this fashion. Although the lifting is a physical task, psychological factors play the major role.

As you think about being lifted, you begin to tense those muscles that make it easier for others to lift you. There are no real changes in your body weight, only in your muscle tone and in how your weight is distributed. As neck and shoulder muscles tense, the body becomes rigid and more elongated. This causes the people lifting you to be able to get underneath your center of gravity and to be able to use the strength in both their arms and legs to pick you up. In contrast, when you think *down*, there is a redistribution of weight downward. Your knees bend slightly and your arms and shoulders are lowered as you think of reaching down through the floor. This thinking *down* unconsciously results in a lowering of the center of gravity, this time forcing the people doing the lifting to rely more on arm muscles since they can no longer push straight up. In addition your change in posture results in the people on either side pushing in toward each other, nullifying their strength rather than combining their strength to lift.

I want to emphasize that there is no trick or deception involved in the demonstrations just mentioned. They illustrate, irrefutably, that thought and movement are related, and I hope it's becoming apparent that anyone engaging in competitive athletics should certainly take the time to analyze the relationship between thought and movement in his own sport. This is an absolute necessity if he expects to be able to maximize his performance.

For starters, anyone who wants to function at his best must first identify the physical and mental demands of his particular event. Once these are recognized, it's possible to train your mind and body to work together in order to meet those demands. In the past, heavy emphasis on the physical aspects of athletics resulted in many athletes having an inaccurate perception of the demands of their sport. Their reliance on strength alone inevitably caused early fatigue, and if it continued, it usually resulted in early retirement. Pitchers just coming into the big leagues provide a classic example. Most young pitchers are very strong and some of them rely on a great fast ball and little else. If they plan to stay in the big leagues, they learn to use their heads as well as their arms. They also learn new pitches which require less strength. As an example, pitchers like Hoyt Wilhelm didn't come in throwing knuckle balls; they learned to pitch them in order to survive.

Returning to the martial arts, we can see that the masters' integrated abilities enabled them to perform feats which really do seem to border on the superhuman. In fact the demands made on athletes may pall by comparison, although this is not to say that a karate expert can outshoot Rick Barry or steal bases like Joe Morgan. Still, there have been extraordinary feats involving great strength, coordination, timing, and concentration performed by the masters. Oyama, a karate practitioner, has fought and killed a bull with his bare hands. Uyeshiba, the founder of aikido, is reported to have dodged bullets. And I have seen experts in actual fights (not just demonstrations) take on several people at the same time. The late Bruce Lee, of movie fame, wasn't the only one-man army in town.

As you read the following examples, try to imagine yourself in the situations being described. Think of the thoughts, feelings, and reactions that *you* would be having under similar conditions and think of how they would interfere with your performance. To the extent that you are able to accomplish this, you will begin to get a feeling for the tremendous control masters of the martial arts learn to exert over mental processes.

For the sake of high drama, let's consider the Uyeshiba example first. In the 1930s Uyeshiba was journeying through China when his caravan was attacked by a group of bandits intent upon robbing and killing Uyeshiba and his companions. As Uyeshiba later related it, a bandit was pointing a pistol at him, and just before he actually fired, the master of aikido experienced a "spiritual bullet," which caused him first to pivot to the side and then move in toward his attacker. Once he had reached a position alongside the attacker, it was a simple matter to execute a takedown and disarm the man.

The physical requirements on Uyeshiba in this situation were not that demanding. Most adult males are between eighteen and twenty inches wide from shoulder to shoulder. If a gun is pointed at the center of the chest, a move of only ten inches to the side is enough to get the person completely out of the line of fire. *The trick is to be able to move at an appropriate time and without warning your attacker.* Uyeshiba spoke of a "spiritual bullet" passing through him before the gun was actually fired. It was this "spiritual bullet" that caused him to act at that precise moment. One way of conceptualizing the "spiritual bullet" he was describing is to view it as the sum of all the cues that are available warning one that a gun is about to be fired.

When a gun is fired, there is a loud bang as the powder explodes. The individual firing the gun anticipates the bang by up to a second before he completely pulls the trigger. This anticipation results in wrinkles in the forehead and visible changes in the muscle tension in the temples and around the ears. In addition, when firing a pistol, there is a tendency to pull down on the weapon just prior to the explosion in order to compensate for the upward jump of the handgun as it is fired. All these cues, which occur in advance of the actual firing, are available to a trained observer and provide surprisingly ample warning that the gunman is about to fire.

Uyeshiba apparently was able to maintain sufficient presence of mind while being attacked to observe these cues. Despite generations of Western movies and TV serials, this is the sort of Academy Award performance of which very few of us are capable. Most of us would respond with our minds becoming a blank or with our attention completely rooted on some irrelevant stimulus like the gaping hole in the end of the pistol barrel. This response would keep us from picking up on, and responding to, the cues indicating the gunman was about to fire.

In explaining how it's possible to dodge bullets, it's important to have some understanding of the actual speed in which a mere mortal can react to a sudden move. Under optimal conditions it would have taken the gunman at least one-tenth of a second to begin to respond to Uyeshiba's first move, provided Uyeshiba made the move without telegraphing it in the same way the gunman telegraphed his intent to fire. In that one-tenth of a second, the master could have moved at least two feet. As was pointed out earlier, a movement of only ten inches would have been sufficient to get him out of the line of fire. Once the gunman began to react, he must have attempted to catch up with the changed situation. Since by this time the master had moved in close enough to disarm him, it was already too late.

It sounds unlikely, I know, but as with the breaking of a one-inch board, most healthy individuals between the ages of sixteen and fifty can duplicate Uyeshiba's feat with only a minimum of training. The physical demands are really quite minor. Realistically, however, most of us would be psychologically unable to observe the situation to our advantage; we would be paralyzed into inaction through our own fears and thoughts.

Without the potentially deadly consequences, similar situations arise in athletic competition all the time. Boxers telegraph the punches they are going to throw, linemen the moves they will make, quarterbacks where they intend to pass, and so on. Most of these warning signals can be used to our advantage, but they go unobserved because our attention is directed elsewhere. Too often we are so caught up in thinking about ourselves and our own moves that we don't bother to notice what our opponent is doing. The example just presented demanded that Uyeshiba be able to focus his attention and energy on the one gunman. There are times, however, when such an intense and narrow attentional focus would be inappropriate.

Frequently, as part of a demonstration, masters of the martial arts illustrate their ability to cope with several attackers at the same time. Perhaps some of the most amazing demonstrations of this kind were those put on by Master Uyeshiba until he was well into his eighties. I was in Japan in the early 1960s, when the Master was already that old, and was privileged to witness one of these demonstrations—which reminded me, to a degree, of those quickness drills used by football coaches to teach their players to cope with more than one opponent at a time.

As in the football drills, Master Uyeshiba was surrounded by five to seven attackers whose task was to take him by surprise. They charged at him, either individually or in groups, and tried to knock him down. To this onlooker, Uyeshiba seemed to glide around inside the circle, and as his attackers came at him, he effortlessly escaped their clutches with movements that were smooth and almost dancelike. In some ways he reminded me of a brilliant bullfighter as he worked in slow motion in contrast to the fierce all-out movements of his attackers—except that in this case the master got hold of his attackers and tossed them, while they, like the frustrated bull, were never able to grab hold of him. In fact most of them never even touched him. He used small, subtle body movements to get them to come on even faster, like blitzing linebackers. Then he helped them on their way out of the circle, or else he completely evaded them and they became victims of their own momentum as they tripped over themselves and went crashing out of the circle.

Uyeshiba's movements and his use of an opponent's own charge to defeat him are seen in athletic situations all the time. A defensive lineman may lean as he charges in. The blocker, noticing this, simply steps aside, and as the lineman charges past, the blocker gives him a quick shove on his back. This shove is just enough to cause the lineman to lose his balance and fall. The same kind of situation occurs in basketball. In a one-on-one situation the man with the ball fakes a shot, causing the man guarding him to jump up and lean forward in an attempt to block the shot. While the person is up in the air and leaning, he is extremely vulnerable. Should the individual with the ball drive for the basket and happen to bump into his opponent's legs, he may cause him to have a bad fall. The slight push added to the self-initiated movement of the player attempting to block the shot is enough to make him completely lose control of his body.

As with other examples it is useful to examine both the physical and psychological demands associated with fighting several individuals at the same time. In the Uyeshiba demonstration, speed and strength are not that important. This has to be true because even a superbly conditioned eighty-year-old man like Uyeshiba is not going to have the speed and strength of the average twenty-five-year-old. Obviously a knowledge of some basic moves in response to attack are needed. Uyeshiba had to know a variety of pivots, blocks, and throwing techniques and had to be able to execute them perfectly, without hesitation or conscious thought. What is most critical is the timing and coordination of the moves, however, rather than the strength involved. The particular techniques must be practiced until they are as graceful as a dance, and the timing, particularly since the strength involved is minimal, must be exact. To move too early or too late would have placed Uyeshiba in a position of having to meet the strength of his opponent, quite literally, head on. This would have been a battle which at his age he most probably would have lost.

As for the psychological demands that accompany the act of fighting several people at the same time, the individual defending himself must be able to maintain a very broad, evenly distributed focus of attention. If the athlete in the center of the circle focuses and maintains all his attention on any one of his opponents, he is unable to respond to movements made by others in the circle. Likewise, if thoughts and fears about the situation he finds himself in (for example, "How did I get into this?") demand his attention, then he becomes distracted and loses the ability to perform effectively. Finally, if he has to stop mentally and think about what he's doing, he isn't able to react quickly enough to the movements of his attackers. To say the least, his is not a simple task.

Happily, although the psychological demands placed on the person being attacked are difficult to meet, there are also some psychological factors that can work to his advantage. In some ways it's actually easier to fight more than one person at a time than to have to deal with a single individual. When the odds are three or four to one, there's a tendency for the attackers to be less vigilant than they ought to be. They feel confident and relaxed because experience has led the individuals with the advantage to believe that they won't be challenged. This is particularly true in a fighting situation for those individuals who believe they are out of the line of sight of the person they are attacking. Because of this reduction in vigilance, they become vulnerable to a sudden move in their direction. Because they anticipate little resistance to any move they initiate, they tend to commit themselves to one move at a time, not faking first and not preparing for a countermove by their opponent.

Because of the above factors the person in the circle can often easily overcome one or two of his first attackers. This demonstration of both skill and "cool" is usually enough to raise the anxiety level of the remaining opponents and results in an impairment in their ability to function effectively. To return to athletics, the same thing occurs when one team relaxes because it has a big lead and lets down its guard; the other team makes a go of it and suddenly it's a new ball game. Often the shock is such that the team which originally led is unable to come back. The team members become anxious, tighten up, begin to make mistakes, and lose the game.

Scientists, as will be shown later, are just beginning to become aware of the tremendous control individuals are capable of exerting over themselves. Apart from the illustrations already presented, some of the masters of the martial arts evidence such control over mental and physical processes that occasionally things they do seem to defy rational explanation. This is particularly true when they demonstrate control over their physical responsivity to pain or their resistance to the effects that drugs such as alcohol might be expected to have on them. It's worthwhile to look closely at these abilities, for to the extent that it's possible to understand the functions involved, it becomes possible to use what is learned to enhance performance.

While in Japan studying the martial arts, I watched a demonstration in which my instructor was to take a knife away from an attacker. The knife used in this sort of demonstration is very sharp, and the technique requires that the defender pivot in a half-circle to the outside just as the attacker thrusts the knife at his stomach. In conjunction with the pivot, the defender's hand comes across the top of the attacker's arm and then slides down to catch the knife hand behind the wrist. When this is done successfully, the defender then pivots back to his original position. This movement causes him to twist the opponent's knife hand up and out, placing a great deal of pressure on the wrist and forcing him to drop the knife. Unfortunately in this particular demonstration my instructor did not get a firm hold on his opponent's wrist, and the knife hand was pulled back, slicing his palm wide open. From my position just off to the side I was unable to see any indication of pain or surprise on his face. Instead, apparently oblivious to what had happened, he executed another 180-degree pivot, which placed him behind his attacker and allowed him to deliver a blow to the back of the opponent's neck. Once this had been accomplished, he walked calmly to the side and wrapped a cloth bandage around his hand. Then without any evidence of pain he returned to complete the demonstration.

On another occasion, the instructor performed an equally memorable, albeit very different feat. A number of us had been to a party at which the instructor drank sake to the point of passing out. We more or less had to carry him as we left the party. I draped one of his arms around my shoulder and another student did the same. Our instructor was completely limp, with his feet dragging between us. We were walking back toward a bus station when someone stepped out into the street about a hundred feet in front of us. It was very dark and there was no one else in sight. The person in the street yelled, challenging us to a fight. At that point it was as if an electric current had suddenly passed through our instructor's body. Somehow, even though I'm certain he was unconscious from the alcohol, he had maintained enough awareness to react to this challenge. He stood up, pushed us aside, and literally charged off in the direction of our challenger.

As luck would have it, the challenge came from a fellow student. He was feeling his oats as a result of all the alcohol he had consumed, but when he realized who was rushing at him, he became very frightened and started apologizing profusely. At that point we all began to laugh at the humor of the situation. We laughed even harder as we watched our instructor quietly pass out once again.

The ability to be aware of special things going on around you and to be able to react to them even though apparently unconscious is indeed difficult to explain. A similar story told about Master Uyeshiba involves an attempt made by some of his students to take him by surprise. In his demonstrations and in practice sessions, Uyeshiba was so agile that his students were literally unable to grab him and hold on. He never seemed to be where they reached. Like a great boxer slipping punches, he seemed to effortlessly move just enough to have them pass harmlessly off to the side. One evening a group of his students decided that they would try to sneak up on him while he was asleep. They waited outside his room until they heard sounds like sleeping, then they slowly began to open the door to his room. Immediately they heard him say, "Who's there?" They stopped, retreated to a safe distance, and waited until they again thought he was asleep. Once more they attempted to sneak into the room and again they were greeted by the same question. This procedure went on all night with the students being unable to enter. The next morning at practice they were amazed to see a very refreshed instructor who indicated that he had had a very peaceful rest and had, in fact, slept undisturbed.

The ability of the mind to become attuned to certain cues and of the individual to respond to these cues in spite of physical impairment is not completely understood. Sometimes a mother, home from the hospital, exhausted after childbirth and on medication to help her sleep, still wakes up to small changes in the breathing pattern of her baby. Apparently all her mental energy is directed toward the awareness of a few very important stimuli. She sleeps undisturbed by cars, trucks, trains, and sounds of the night, but the cry of the baby immediately awakens her. In a similar way, through his years of training, Uyeshiba must have been able to control his attention. He must have trained himself to be very sensitive to unusual cues and to ignore many others.

We know so much, yet we know so little. We can't explain all the phenomena cited in this chapter, yet we do have explanations for some of these occurrences. In addition to the explanations already postulated, studies and case reports from the literature on hypnosis provide an understanding of some of the other factors involved. For example, with selected subjects it's possible to use hypnotic suggestions to control responsivity to pain. In fact prior to the availability of general anesthesia thousands of major surgical procedures were performed using hypnosis as the only anesthetic. In the 1800s a Scottish physician named Edsdaile is reported to have performed over 300 operations for the removal of scrotal tumors, using hypnosis as the only anesthesia. His success with the surgery was far greater than that of other surgeons using chemical forms of anesthesia. In fact his mortality rate for this particular surgery was only five per cent, far below the fifty per cent death rate of the other surgeons.[4]

We'll get into hypnotic suggestion at some length later in the book, but it does bear mentioning here that hypnosis, in addition to its use as an anesthesia in childbirth, dentistry, surgery, and even terminal illnesses, has also been used to stop premature labor, remove warts, and both treat and ease skin rashes—the latter merely being a demonstration of hypnotic suggestion rather than any kind of beneficial usage. Suffice it to say at this point in the book that in each instance nothing more than some verbal suggestions administered by a hypnotist was sufficient to cause dramatic physiological changes—and hypnosis is but one method of suggestion used to alter the mental and physical functioning of an individual. We'll also learn later on that meditative procedures similar to those used by practitioners of the martial arts, by Zen priests, and by yogis have been shown to have what seem to us rather amazing physiological effects on the individual. Each of these procedures seems to work by assisting the individual to direct and control his attention or thought processes. Through different training procedures, the individual learns to direct attention away from painful stimuli and to ignore them, thus increasing both his pain threshold and his tolerance of pain.

For that matter, instances of a high threshold of pain and a rather startling tolerance to it are not that uncommon in Western athletics. Athletes, particularly in contact sports, occasionally play for long periods of time without being aware of major injuries. It is becoming increasingly apparent that under these conditions the mental attitude of the individual is such that his awareness is directed away from the pain. Sometimes this results from emotional shock; other times it is simply due to the strength of the demands for attention made by other cues in the competitive environment. What's very important here is that it's possible to bring this under the individual's voluntary control by teaching him to gain greater control over his attentional processes.

My intent in discussing the martial arts in such detail has been to use them to provide illustrations of some of the feats that are possible through the integration of mental and physical functioning. The exciting promise for you, the athlete, is that through gaining control over mental processes, you gain additional control over your physical abilities and thus perform at a higher level. In the next chapter some of the psychological variables that must be learned are spelled out in more detail.

Chapter Two. **Attention in Athletics**

In describing some of the remarkable feats performed by the martial arts masters, I placed considerable emphasis on their ability to control mental processes, which in turn allows them to perform at levels many of us only dream of. A man like Uyeshiba appears to be able to focus his attention completely—that is, he can focus all of his thought processes and energy in a particular direction. Such a focus demands total concentration. While directing his thoughts and energy in this manner, he shuts himself off from anything that might be a distraction. All of us at one time or another find ourselves maintaining so narrow a focus that we become oblivious to everything around us. Usually this is not something we try to do. We just fall into it.

Although such a narrow focus of attention can be useful in attempting to accomplish a particular act, such as hitting a baseball or breaking a board, it can also be detrimental. Remember Uyeshiba and the circle of attackers—he couldn't concentrate on just one of them. If the competitive situation we find ourselves in demands that we be ready to respond to a number of possibilities, a narrow focus is most inappropriate. For example, a pitcher with a runner on base must remember to look him back to the bag as well as attend to the catcher and to the position of his outfield.

A humorous example of an inappropriately narrow focus of attention occurred on the opening kickoff of the 1976 Super Bowl. Reggie Harrison, a member of the Pittsburgh Steelers specialty team, was supposed to run downfield and hit the outside corner of the Dallas blocking wedge. In talking to a reporter after the game, he said, "I was so charged up, I went downfield flying, screaming and yelling at the top of my lungs. I yelled so much, I forgot my duty." Dallas ran the kick back to the Pittsburgh 45.

Recognizing that a constant narrow focus would be bad, masters of the martial arts instruct students to learn to narrow and broaden attention at will. To broaden the focus, you have to let your mind "touch everything evenly." And once you can do this, you become far more aware of any significant changes in your surroundings and are able to respond properly. As we'll see, in fast-moving team sports, such as basketball, hockey, football, and baseball, the ability to broaden attention at will is crucial.

Width of Attention

Most of us are capable of moving from a fairly narrow focus, such as reading a book, to a fairly broad focus such as driving a car in busy city traffic. But we differ from the martial arts practitioners in two significant ways. First, we cannot sustain either the narrow or broad focus. Secondly, and more importantly, we have less ability to voluntarily control the movement of our attention along the narrow-broad focus that I have described. For us full control over attention occurs only by accident or in ideal situations.

Obviously our ability to control width of attention has some important bearing on our ability to perform effectively in competitive situations. This is true whether we are bowling, golfing, or simply playing touch football. However, as important as attentional width is in explaining some aspects of an athlete's performance, it's not the only dimension.

Direction of Attention

In addition to thinking about your attention as being either broad or narrow, you should also think of it as having direction. At any given point in time your attention is directed to either external or internal stimuli. When you have an internally directed focus of attention, you're involved in your own thoughts and feelings. For example, you might be concentrating on your heartbeat or thinking about the solution to a particular problem. You might be brooding over something that happened in the past or something you believe will happen in the future. The important point is that at that particular instant your attention is directed internally, and as a consequence, for a brief period of time you lose awareness of what is going on around you. By contrast, when you focus externally you are attending to objects and events that are outside your own body, and you are no longer in contact with your thoughts and feelings. At this time your responses to the environment occur at a reflexive level without any conscious decisions being made on your part. For example, you react to someone throwing something at you by ducking. You don't think about it first, you simply respond.

Just as width of attention can be described on a continuum, so can the direction of your attention focus. Under most circumstances we attempt to maintain a balance between attending to external processes (environment) and internal processes (thoughts, feelings, ideas). This is because the majority of competitive situations require that we shift from an internal focus to an external focus very rapidly. As an example, if you are a pitcher, you develop an internal focus in order to decide how to pitch to a particular batter; then you shift your attention to external stimuli (the catcher's mitt) in order to pitch. Should your strategy change after the pitch, you go back to an internal focus. As a general rule, the more complex and rapidly changing the situation, the more externally focused your attention must be. And conversely, as the need for analysis or planning increases, the more internal and reflective your focus becomes.

Because most of us have problems controlling our width of attention, we also experience difficulty sustaining a directional focus when we need to, or we have difficulty shifting the direction of our focus. In competition, as the environment becomes more stressful, our ability to control both the width and direction of attention decreases even more. It's under these conditions that we either "choke" or "come through in the clutch."

An understanding of your particular attentional style can be used to help explain your past successes and failures in competitive situations.[1] In addition your attentional style can be used to predict how you will perform under a variety of new situations. The idea that your success and failure can be predicted on the basis of your attentional processes implies that your ability to control the width and direction of attention is constant across competitive situations.

Width and Direction

I want to emphasize that for analyzing a particular moment in time, it is important to think of attention on the basis of both its width and direction. This point can be clarified by

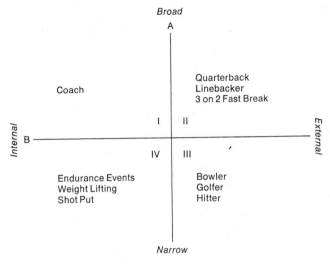

Figure 2.1   Attentional Focus

examining Figure 2.1. As the figure illustrates, width of attention is indicated by a perpendicular line, with a broad focus at the top and a narrow focus at the bottom. Presumably we all fall at different places on this line, but you may spend most of your time at the top. Because of this tendency you would have a broad focus, and we would find you at A. By contrast, if you're the type of person who spends most of his time wrapped up in his thoughts, you would have an internal style and we would locate you at B on the horizontal line, which represents the direction of our attention.

The figure that the two attentional variables create can be divided into four parts. Part I at the top left represents a broad-internal attentional focus. People with this sort of style ponder and think about a variety of things and may continue to do so even when the situation demands other types of attention. On the other hand, the ability to have a broad-internal focus is important for a coach. Formulating a game plan and mentally comparing various players' skills in order to make substitutions requires this kind of thinking.

Part II of the figure, a broad-external style, represents the type of attention you need in order to respond to complex and rapidly changing situations. A quarterback, who must pick out primary and secondary receivers while he avoids getting sacked, and a basketball player leading a fast break are two examples of athletes who need to be able to maintain this type of attention.

The third quadrant describes a narrow-external type of attention. This particular attentional focus is useful when you must respond to very few cues and if the physical behavior you are engaging in, once initiated, can continue without modification. For example, once a golf swing is initiated, it becomes an unconscious, automatic process. Sports such as golf, bowling, tennis, and most track and field events require this type of attention.

The fourth quadrant represents a narrow-internal focus. Athletes such as distance runners and swimmers, who do not have to respond to rapid or sudden environmental changes, often use this type of focus to increase their endurance and tolerance for pain. These athletes are able to develop a particular thought or rhythm and then to lock onto it. This ability allows them to ignore a great deal of fatigue and pain, and it keeps them from developing self-defeating thoughts and attitudes.

Most of us, as we feel fatigue and pain, begin to find ourselves trapped in the vicious cycle I referred to earlier. We don't want to feel tired or be hurting, because this means we may have to stop what we are doing or we may lose. This conflict between physical feelings and the mental desire to continue results in thoughts like, "I may not make it," and "Man, am I tired!" These thoughts, if they suggest or even hint at possible failure, produce increases in muscle tension, which in turn accent the feeling of fatigue and increase the pain.

An interviewer once asked Mark Spitz how he kept this downward spiral from developing. The interviewer was particularly interested in how he could keep going lap after lap in practice despite being on the verge of exhaustion. Spitz responded by saying that he imagined a different girl at each end of the pool, waiting for him with open arms. He swam from one girl to the other, and if his times decreased, it simply reflected the attractiveness of the girl rather than his fatigue. Without analyzing what this particular strategy says about Mark Spitz's interests, we have to admit that it's an effective way of avoiding the development of self-defeating thoughts for those athletes who need to narrow their attention.

To reemphasize a point, most of us are able to move along both of the attentional dimensions described, and at different times may find ourselves in each of the quadrants described. However, our ability to move in a particular direction at a given time varies, and unless we're able to function on the level of a master of the martial arts, we won't be able to move equally well in all directions. This is particularly true under competitive conditions. Because of past learning, level of motivation, and/or heredity, an athlete may be able to develop a broad-internal focus quite easily and yet have difficulty developing a narrow-external one. Each of us spends more time with the attentional focus that was easiest for him to develop. This preference gives us different strengths and weaknesses in different competitive situations. For example, some golfers possess the narrow attentional focus necessary to concentrate on a shot but have difficulty broadening attention when the situation requires it. This type of golfer has trouble selecting the appropriate club because of the many factors involved (e.g., distance, wind, his own strength that day, or the heaviness of the air).

The Analytical Athlete

Athletes who tend to have a broad-internal attentional style can be described as analytical. These individuals are good at absorbing information—they often play the game in their head prior to the actual competition and then replay it afterward. On the field of play they rarely make the same mistake twice and they're able to overcome a poor start by being flexible enough to adjust their style of play. In addition, because of their attentional style they are able to analyze the moves of their opponents and can often predict in advance what their competition will do next.

Perversely enough, just as this analytical tendency can be a source of great strength, it can also be a major weakness. For example, such athletes have a tendency to outguess themselves. A hitter in baseball decides the next pitch will be a curve and readies himself to react to a curve. When the pitcher throws a fast ball instead, the hitter doesn't even get the bat off his shoulder. Analytical individuals can become so preoccupied with their analysis that they lose awareness of what's going on around them. We've all seen the end in football who is so busy thinking about the wonderful pattern he's going to run that he fails to hear the signal to snap the ball.

The Quarterback

The second type of attentional style an individual may have is a broad-external one. This focus is ideal for reacting to competitive situations which are rapidly changing and involve a large physical area. Athletes with a broad-external focus seem to be aware of everything that is going on around them. A good base runner knows if the shortstop is trying to sneak in behind him. He is aware of the positions of other players and knows what to do when something happens. A top linebacker has to be proficient at adjusting to shifts in the offensive backfield. A winning quarterback picks up his secondary receivers if his primary receiver is covered. In basketball and hockey this type of player always seems to be able to spot the open man.

Problems occur when an athlete with a broad-external focus takes in so much irrelevant information he becomes overloaded and confused. For instance, the quarterback who has just completed a short pass on third and eight finds himself with very short yardage on the fourth down. He decides to call a quarterback sneak, and his attentional focus, which spanned all his receivers on the previous play, must now be narrowed to the problem at hand—getting that yardage for the first down. However, he's already thinking about the pass play he's going to call on the next play—visualizing the secondary coverage, etc.—and he fumbles the pass from center.

Keep Your Eye on the Ball

The more precise an athletic movement must be, the narrower the attention focused on it. The third attentional style, a narrow-external focus, is ideal in those situations where optimal performance requires total concentration on a particular point or object. Putting in golf, target and trap shooting, field-goal kicking, bowling, and broad jumping are all examples of events that require competitors to have a narrow-external attentional focus. Athletes capable of maintaining this type of attention have the ideal style for avoiding distraction due to irrelevant stimuli. For example, their ability to narrow attention means they are not bothered by crowd noises or spectators being close by. In addition, the external direction of their attention also keeps them from becoming distracted by their own internal thoughts, feelings, and fears. Reggie Jackson epitomizes this style when he says he concentrates so intently at the plate he doesn't know if the pitcher is right- or left-handed.

As with any inflexible type of attention, problems occur when the environmental situation is one that demands flexibility and change. For example, if the quarterback in a football game has a narrow focus and his primary receiver is covered, he fails to pick out the secondary receiver. While he's concentrating on his primary receiver, he's likely to be tackled for a loss or throw an interception. The errors that occur with this attentional style are errors of underinclusion. They occur because the athlete reacts without having enough information. Some other examples of underinclusive errors are the fielder who catches the fly and then fails to cut off the base runner, or the basketball player who is so intent on the man in front of him that he fails to hear the player behind him, who steals the ball. A star like Walt Frazier loves this type of opponent.

I Am a Rock

The final quadrant in the attentional diagram describes those athletes who have a predominantly narrow-internal attentional style. Such people find it easy to direct their attention inward and to lock onto a single thought or feeling. This ability can be very helpful to athletes engaging in endurance events or in events that demand one intense surge of power (shot putting, weight lifting). By being able to maintain attention on a single thought or feeling, a runner can develop a rhythm that will help increase both endurance and pain tolerance. The explanation for this is that the real physiological pain he is experiencing is heightened by the psychological pain, and this can be dealt with or eliminated. The psychological aspect of pain can be controlled by individuals who are capable of directing attention in a very narrowly focused way. This is accomplished by narrowing attention so that the focus is on nonpainful stimuli. Through this focus, conscious awareness—and thus the experience of pain—disappears or is reduced.

Such a redirection of attention to reduce pain has been employed by dentists, hypnotists, and meditators. Dentists play music or use the sound of running water as a means of directing attention away from the pain. Hypnotists verbally suggest and direct the subject to attend to different stimuli. Meditators, through practice, can learn to direct their own attention away from painful stimuli by focusing on a particular thought or feeling. Some athletes accomplish the same feat by narrowing their attention and focusing on certain body functions such as movement of their legs, the swing of their arms, or the rhythm of their breathing.

In a similar way those athletes with a narrow-internal style seem better able to push themselves and to stay involved with practice in spite of distractions. A pretty co-ed comes to watch practice, for example, but she doesn't turn any heads. It's not that the players don't like to date pretty girls but rather that dating just doesn't enter their minds. Their concentration is so intense that they don't notice the girl. Since she is not noticed, she is not distracting—which may bother *her* just a little.

As with other attentional styles, the major strength of this particular style is also its major weakness. Although a narrow-internal focus can be used to motivate and increase tolerance to pain, it can also have the opposite effect. Consider two swimmers, both with a narrow-internal style of attention. The first swimmer has a good self-concept and thinks of swimming against the world record each race. This swimmer uses this imagery to push himself harder. The second swimmer, however, has a low self-concept. Every time he gets on the blocks, he asks his competitor what his best time for the event is. On those occasions when the time is better than his own, he is swamped with thoughts of failure and defeat. The result is that he becomes anxious, tightens up, and can't swim up to his capacity. Both swimmers have a narrow attentional style, but for one it's a curse rather than a blessing.

So far I have talked about attention as though it is always categorized by one of the four quadrants discussed. Clearly this is not the case. As a competitive situation becomes more complex or as the game or meet progresses, many different attentional styles may develop. One example: to select a club for a golf shot, you may first need a broad-external focus in order to be aware of all of the things such as distance, lie, position of traps, wind, etc., which will affect your selection. Next you need a broad internal focus in order to integrate this information with what you know about your own past performance under similar conditions, with the relative importance of the particular shot (play safe or take a chance), and with how you feel physically at that point in time. Through analysis of this information you select the proper club. Then your attention must narrow and focus externally on the ball. After the shot you may wish to use a narrow-internal focus to replay what happened (for example, how you felt while shooting) in order to become aware of any mistakes you might have made. And so on.

As you can see, flexibility of attention is vital. Errors occur when your flexibility breaks down. For most of us there is a consistency to the type of error we make because we have difficulty developing one or more of the four styles described. This means we often enter a competitive situation with the wrong attentional style. In the example above, if we had difficulty developing a narrow-internal focus, we would not be able to recognize the mistakes which we made on a particular shot. Thus we couldn't correct for a slice because we wouldn't know what caused it. Likewise, if we could not narrow our external focus, we would be distracted by our own irrelevant thoughts or by crowd sounds when trying to putt.

Obviously the purer and less flexible your attentional style, the more difficulty you have adapting to changing conditions. Each of us has to recognize our attentional limitations. One way of doing this is by becoming aware of the types of errors which occur because of some specific attentional deficit.

Hothead

If you're the type of person who has a predominantly external attentional focus, you're likely to respond to competitive situations in a reflexive or on-the-spot way. The purer the direction of your attention to external stimuli, the more difficulty you have in sticking to your pregame plan or your prerace strategy. In other words a dominant external focus means that you're reacting to the situation as though you're being exposed to it for the first time. With this focus you fail to learn from your mistakes, and opponents can take advantage of this by continually suckering you into making the same errors.

Coaches with a dominant external focus lose their "cool" during the game. They react to unexpected happenings impulsively or without thinking, and the analytical component of their game plan falls by the wayside. Quite obviously what happens here is that the coach fails to focus internally. This failure keeps him from using past situations to modify present behavior or to predict what will happen in the future, until it's too late. In terms of personality, large mood fluctuations accompany a predominantly external focus. When things are going well, the coach is patting everyone on the back, even those who are not performing well. On the other hand, when things don't seem to be working out, the coach gives everyone hell. This behavior creates problems since the feedback the athlete gets is often unrelated to his actual performance. In effect he may be getting praised for performing poorly and punished for doing a good job. To say the very least, such a situation makes it difficult to develop trust and respect for the coach's judgment.

Mr. Cool

Some of us have just the opposite problem. We tend to have a dominant internal focus. We may spend so much time inside our own heads that we fail to notice what is going on around us. We may begin with an external focus, noticing a particular problem, and then spend the next few minutes planning a strategy for dealing with it. Unfortunately, by the time we are ready to implement the changes, the situation has changed and our strategy is no longer appropriate. Depending upon how observant we are, we may either go ahead with the useless strategy or we may drift off, planning another strategy to deal with the new problem.

Coaches with this difficulty run into problems with their athletes because they are not attentive to what the athletes are actually doing. The coach is so busy thinking about his own reactions and what he is saying to his team that he doesn't notice how the players are responding. The result is that he becomes insensitive to the needs of his players. In addition the coach's internal focus may act to inhibit his expression of emotions. Thus the athletes he coaches often get the feeling that the coach doesn't much care about them as individuals.

Those of us with an internal focus often use our attentional style as a means of controlling our emotions. We think and analyze to such a degree that we literally think away any feelings. This logical "cool," though it may keep us out of arguments and fights, can also cause difficulties. People we deal with begin to feel that they must be unimportant to us since they don't seem to be able to get us to react emotionally. Obviously there are times when you need to be able to maintain your "cool." At the same time, particularly when trying to work with other people, it's important that some feelings are shared. Coaches and players with respect for each other and with different styles can complement each other nicely and can teach each other to overcome their faults.

Chicken Little or Mr. Indecisive

The second dimension of attention that I talked about, that of width, can also influence your ability to function over time. If you're the type of person who has a broad focus (both external and internal) and who has difficulty narrowing attention, then you have a special set of problems. With a broad focus there is often a tendency to attempt to deal with more things than are necessary. In preparing for a game, you may attempt to anticipate all the possible things which might happen, and this can result in your spreading practice too thin in an attempt to cover too many contingencies. When this occurs, basic fundamentals are sacrificed, and you end up being "jock" of all trades and a master of none.

Like the athlete with an external focus, the individual with too broad a focus has difficulty sticking to a game plan. The difference between these two styles is that the individual with a broad focus is able to develop plans but then jumps from plan to plan. By contrast, if his attention is always directed externally, he reacts without any plan at all.

As with any dominant attentional style, a broad attentional focus can lead to interpersonal problems. As an example, a coach with a broad focus is likely to take a player who has already developed a high degree of skill and try to change him. Consider the coach who has a basketball player who has consistently made eighty per cent of his free throws. During one game the player has a bad night at the free-throw line. The coach watches this failure, analyzes what the player is doing, and tells him to move his hand farther down, under the ball. Instead of recognizing that some situational influences—or simply bad luck—may have been interfering with the player's performance, the coach overreacts or overcoaches. Under these conditions, if the player follows the coach's suggestions, the result can be disastrous—more bad nights at the foul line.

Finally, verbal individuals with a broad attentional focus can confuse others with the sheer weight of their ideas and talk. They offer so many suggestions and alternatives that they cloud issues rather than clarify them.

I'm Dedicated—or I Can't See the Forest for the Trees

When attention is dominated by a narrow focus, an athlete may make mistakes because he does not consider enough alternatives and because he reacts to only part of a problem. An individual with such a style may be content to practice a few moves to the nth degree. Naturally enough, if his opponent happens to be vulnerable to the moves practiced, he performs very well. But against a new alignment or situation, he lacks the flexibility to develop and try a new strategy.

People with a narrow focus can also have interpersonal problems since they have difficulty in recognizing and adapting to the needs and styles of other people. I had a diving coach who made every diver on the team practice pointing his toes on a hurdle step for an hour, even though it was a problem for only one member of the team. In this situation the rest of us became angry and bored.

In the same way that attention can be analyzed on the basis of width and direction of focus, competitive situations can be understood in terms of the demands they place on our attentional processes. If, by chance or by design, width and direction of focus match these demands, performance will approach optimal levels. For example, if a golfer who naturally has a narrow-external focus finds himself in a putting situation, he should perform well. The rest of course is skill.

In contrast, consider the situation in which your normal attentional style is antagonistic to the demands of the com-

Table 2.1   Attentional Demands of Various Competitive Situations

	Broad-External	Narrow-Internal	Narrow-External	Broad-Internal
Baseball				
1. Hitting			Yes	
2. Pitching				
a. Pitch selection				Yes
b. Delivery			Yes	
3. Fielding	Yes		Yes	
4. Stealing	Yes		Yes	
Football				
1. Calling defensive signals	Yes			Yes
2. Calling offensive signals	Yes			Yes
3. Interior lineman			Yes	
4. Quarterback	Yes		Yes	Yes
a. Calling an audible	Yes			
b. Directing an option	Yes			
5. Linebacker	Yes			Yes
6. Kicker			Yes	
Golf				
1. Club selection	Yes	Yes		
2. Execution of the shot			Yes	
Basketball				
1. Free throw			Yes	
2. Fast break	Yes			
3. Outlet pass	Yes			
4. Rebounding	Yes			
Track and Field				
1. Pole vault		Yes	Yes	
2. Long jump		Yes	Yes	
3. High jump		Yes	Yes	
4. Shot put		Yes		
5. Discus		Yes		
6. Hammer		Yes		
7. Javelin		Yes	Yes	
8. Triple jump		Yes	Yes	
9. Sprint			Yes	
10. Middle distance events		Yes	Yes	
11. Distance events		Yes	Yes	

Table 2.1 (Continued)

	Broad-External	Narrow-Internal	Narrow-External	Broad-Internal
Gymnastics				
1. Planning a routine				Yes
2. Execution		Yes	Yes	
Swimming				
1. Sprints			Yes	
2. Middle distance events		Yes	Yes	
3. Distance events		Yes	Yes	
Coaching				
1. Development of basics			Yes	
2. Development of a game plan				Yes
3. Awareness of players' relative strengths and weaknesses	Yes			Yes
4. Ability to anticipate players' responses to instructions, praise, punishment, etc.			Yes	Yes
Tennis				
1. Pregame strategy				Yes
2. Execution of shot			Yes	
Common Competitive Situations Across Sports				
1. Planning pregame strategy				Yes
2. Analysis of own performance				Yes
3. Final burst of energy		Yes	Yes	
4. Analysis of opponent	Yes			Yes
5. Psyching yourself up		Yes		
6. Maintaining motivation		Yes	Yes	
7. Listening to instructions			Yes	
8. Learning a new move		Yes	Yes	
9. Lowering fear (arousal)	Yes		Yes	

Please note: A blank space means *Not indicated* as opposed to *Definitely not.*

petitive situation. The situation requires you to relate what is happening to past experience and/or training, but your narrow-external focus and your inability to shift to a broad-internal focus keep you from accomplishing your task. To help you determine the type of attention you need for various situations, Table 2.1 presents some of the more common competitive situations and their dominant attentional demands.

In the preceding pages I have treated the ability of individuals to select and control both the width and direction of their attention like a personality trait. This means that just as some individuals are characterized as intelligent or honest or hostile, they can also be characterized as broad or narrow, internal or external attenders. To the extent that these attentional traits exist in the individual, any attempt to upgrade his performance must ensure that his attentional style is appropriate to the demands of the competitive situation. In order to do this, we must first be able to assess an individual's attentional style—we must have a way of testing the athlete and then using the results to describe his attentional processes.

In our laboratory at the University of Rochester we have begun to take some major steps in this direction—toward the development of a test which can be used to describe an individual's attentional capabilities. It's my belief that through the use of such a test and through a growing knowledge of the demands of competitive situations, we can teach athletes better attentional control. There are existing strategies and techniques which can be used to help control the width and direction of attention. In addition, when I analyze the individual's attentional "personality," I can give him insights into *why* he has been making mistakes or "choking." Such insights allow him to recognize and avoid situations where he is likely to perform poorly and, conversely, allow him to become more involved in those athletic situations in which he performs well.

All these points are discussed in detail in Chapter 5, and at that time you will be given an opportunity to assess your own attentional style. Before moving into the actual assessment process, however, it's important to point out that everyone's normal attentional style is affected by competitive factors. Anxiety and arousal are natural components of most athletic competitions and have a direct effect on attentional processes. The mere assessment of your attentional style and of the attentional demands of the situation is not enough to predict how you will perform. If you wish to know when to psych yourself up or psych yourself down, it's critical that you first understand how anxiety affects your attentional style.

Chapter Three. **Anxiety and Performance**

As should be obvious by now, practitioners of the martial arts place a great deal of emphasis on being able to remain calm under conditions of extreme stress. Students are told that they must learn to make their mind "like still water." On a calm day the surface of a pond is smooth and unruffled, a natural mirror, but should the water become disturbed, the images reflected by the water become broken and distorted. Experts in the martial arts maintain that fear does to the human mind what a pebble or the wind does to the surface of a pond, that is, it distorts perceptions and makes it almost impossible to react appropriately. When you become frightened or excited, you lose the ability to control your attention. Not only are your abilities diminished, but you actually begin to misperceive the world around you.

In contrast to the emphasis placed on relaxation by masters of the martial arts, there are many Western coaches who believe in quite the opposite approach. My college swimming coach began his campaign to psych us up weeks before a meet. He posted notes, newspaper clippings,

and statistics dealing with our weaknesses and the respective strengths of our opponents. Once the coach actually refused to let anyone on the team eat lunch or dinner
prior to a big swim meet because he wanted us to be "hungry and mean" when we entered the competition. It made
no difference that some of us wouldn't be swimming until
several hours after the start of the meet or that by then we
might be more hungry and weak or hungry and annoyed
than hungry and mean.

Locker room oratory is another familiar device favored
by coaches, especially those who remember the fabled
"win one for the Gipper" speech made by Knute Rockne
before a key game and more or less immortalized by Pat
O'Brien in the movie made about the great Notre Dame
coach. Speeches like this one, true enough, are remembered and cherished by generations of both players and
coaches, but it's equally true that very few coaches are
capable of such genuinely inspiring oratory. Their players
regard their pregame speechmaking as corny or old-
fashioned or just plain ridiculous.

For that matter, coaches do go from the sublime—as
with Rockne—to the ridiculous in their pregame prepping.
Returning to the example of my hungry-and-mean-minded
coach, I remember one conference meet held in 1965
where he managed to top the previous performances in his
own theater of the absurd.

The meet was being held at a school only thirty miles
from our own college, and it was scheduled so that we had
the preliminary competition on Friday afternoon and evening, and the semifinals and finals on Saturday. We all got
on the bus around 10:00 a.m. Friday so that we would be
ready to warm up around 11:30 a.m. Fortunately most of us
had eaten breakfast before getting on the bus. We swam
from noon until about 3:30 p.m., then everyone was sup-

posedly free until 6:30 p.m., when we would warm up for the evening's competition. All the other teams went to the student union to eat and relax. Our coach, however, was dissatisfied with the efforts of those who had swum in the preliminary races, and he decided to punish the whole team to "make us hungry." We went into a park and sat together on the grass without eating until it was time to warm up again. The coach was taking this hungry business quite literally. We finished with Friday's portion of the meet about 11:00 p.m., but on the way home the coach refused to allow us to stop for dinner because in his estimation we had not done as well as we should have.

The next morning, Saturday, the guys slept until 8:30 a.m. and then had to run to catch the bus to go back to the meet. Because we were "lazy and overslept," we missed breakfast. More warmups, the semifinals, then a break followed. I went to the coach and asked for permission to eat. His response was, "No, I want you hungry. I don't want you heavy in the water."

"But coach," I said, "I haven't eaten for two days. The finals aren't until 8:00 p.m. I'm a diver, not a swimmer, and I don't want to be weak on the board."

"Get out of here," he said. "This is a team! It would break discipline and togetherness, if I let you eat." The team ended up taking fourth place that year—we should have been second. I ended up in sixth place in diving, hating the coach, despite the fact that underneath it all he was a nice guy who really believed in this sort of discipline.

Now, years later, I can understand that my swimming coach had no real perception of the impact of mental and emotional factors on performance. He knew that emotional energy was important, but he had no idea about how to direct it in a constructive way. He generated a lot of energy in the form of anger and similar emotions—it was as though he believed that all he needed to do was get the athletes worked up and the rest would take care of itself.

One explanation for the type of behavior displayed by my coach has to do with the known physiological responses of the body to stress. Studies of the physiological reactions of athletes to competitive stress indicate that a large number of changes occur during these periods, including an increase in the flow of adrenalin. Most people, not only coaches, associate the flow of this particular chemical with an increase in strength. We've all heard stories of individuals performing near-impossible feats of strength during emergencies because of the increased flow of adrenalin. As an example, one woman was reported to have carried a large stove out of her burning house, and there are many stories of individuals lifting up one end of a car. This supposed need to get the old adrenalin going has caused many coaches to attempt to arouse their players by methods which are actually counterproductive to good performance.

A second factor behind the psyching-up philosophy which is so prevalent is an implicit assumption that many people make about *other people's* (but not their own) behavior. Many coaches believe that unless an athlete is excited and stirred up, he won't be motivated and his performance will become sloppy and careless. Moreover, this attitude gets reinforced by those coaches who assume that an athlete's quiet, calm appearance indicates an athlete who is not paying attention and/or an athlete who would much rather be somewhere else. For these coaches, an athlete who appears calm and relaxed, rather than one all worked up into competitive fervor, is a danger sign that certain defeat is in store for the team. It doesn't occur to these coaches that occasionally the calm, relaxed athlete is confident of his abilities and that a team of such athletes is confident of its ability to win. If you *know* you're good, you don't need to be psyched up in order to play well.

Obviously we all need a certain amount of muscle tension and arousal just to be able to remain awake and walk around, but how aroused should we be? Who's correct—the coach yelling, "Go, go, go," or the master of the martial arts? Fortunately we're in a position to answer this question.

Some Operational Definitions

For the rest of this book to be meaningful to you, I am going to provide some psychological definitions of important terms. Stress, as I use it, refers to external conditions—in this case, competitive situations—that can lead to increases in an athlete's physiological level of arousal. These increases—e.g., a faster heart rate, rapid breathing, increased perspiration, increased flow of adrenalin—can be scientifically measured under controlled situations right after a game or meet and can also be observed in terms of how they change under conditions that are assumed to induce arousal. For example, we may deduce that an athlete's arousal level has increased because there was an increase in his heart rate when he anticipated going into the game.

Generally speaking, increases in arousal are not going to help the athlete perform better, but there are special situations where, say, a sudden surge of strength is needed. In the same regard, there is no ironclad rule about an individual's response to stress. One man's stress may not be another man's stress. A coach may view his team's playing in a championship game as highly stressful—his reputation as a winning coach may be riding on this game—whereas many of his athletes do not regard the game in the same way. The coach isn't playing, but he's the one with the higher arousal levels. It's no accident that many coaches retire early, and it's unfortunate that some coaches convey their worried attitudes and emotionality to their players.

In addition to the scientific determination of arousal levels, we can also learn whether or not an athlete is negatively aroused by simply watching his performance—if a fine runner's time is slow, he must be tired, perhaps from increased muscle tension or from less efficient breathing. Another method, certainly much less scientifically objective than physiological measurements, is to talk to the athlete and get his personal responses to the stressful situation. If he reveals that he's worried or confused or not performing up to his usual capabilities, he's revealing a high level of anxiety. Put in the most simple terms, the stress produces an increase in arousal that is preventing him from performing well. Anxiety results from his fear of failure, his awareness of poor performance, and his high level of arousal.

The distinctions I am making between stress, arousal, and anxiety are important ones. In talking about stress, I am not merely speaking of the importance placed upon an event but of the negative physiological effects this overemphasis produces. I am not speaking about arousing athletes from their sleep or sexual excitement or just plain being stirred up. Few people outside the psychological field describe or define these terms in the same way, and this is one of the major reasons for confusion. Under controlled conditions all three of these terms exist in a perfectly predictable relationship to each other—that is, stressful conditions always lead to an increase in arousal (physiological changes) and an increase in anxiety (psychological-emotional changes). But human beings are highly individual and marvelously complex, so each athlete has to be treated in terms of his own physiology and personality. As should be mentioned here, an increase in arousal is not always reflected by an increase in anxiety. If that were so, it would be a perfect world in terms of the scientist, but a very imperfect world for the rest of us.

Individual Responses to Stress

Given the happy fact that each athlete is an individual, we can determine that he is suffering from both arousal and anxiety by observing the changes in his performance (perhaps his coordination and timing seem impaired) and by talking to him and analyzing his verbal responses. If he tells us that he's feeling nervous or worried or upset, we can be pretty certain that an increased level of anxiety isn't doing him any good. His anxiety is being expressed in terms of subjective, personal thoughts and feelings that are all negative in terms of good performance. To give you the broad picture of how this works, Table 3.1 lists some of the physical and mental alterations that can occur as a result of stress. Again, we are viewing these changes as negative ones for the athlete.

As you can see from Table 3.1, those symptoms that are objective can be either physically observed or measured. In contrast, those symptoms that are subjective, such as narrowing of attention, feelings of fatigue, and depression, must be inferred either on the basis of an interview or close questioning of the athlete. Obviously this may not be something to do in the middle of a contest, but even a few responses from the athlete can provide important clues to the falloff in his performance.

Table 3.1   Symptoms Associated with Increasing Levels of Arousal

Physical	Mental
Increased heart rate	Narrow attentional focus
Increased blood pressure	Feeling of fatigue
Rapid breathing	Depression
Increased sugar in blood	Dizziness
Fast EEG activity (20–40 cps)	Confusion
Increased perspiration	Feeling of panic
Frequent urination, loose stools	Loss of control
Nervous movements (finger tapping, chewing)	Inability to direct attention width or focus
Increased muscle tension	
Insomnia	
Nausea	
Increased adrenalin	
Pupil dilation	

For instance, we may know something about your individualized physiological and psychological responses to stress because in previous comparable situations, you have responded by developing excessive muscle tension in your shoulder and neck. By contrast, I may respond to a similar situation by developing an upset stomach or stomach cramps. You complain of feeling tense and unable to move well; my complaint is that I'm nervous and afraid of playing poorly. We both are responding to arousal in objective, measurable ways but are expressing our anxiety in subjective terms. As I've said, each athlete is an individual and is going to suffer his own form of anxiety.

In the same manner, each of us has an optimal level of arousal at which we perform best. Physiological changes beyond this level harm rather than help us, but obviously we need to respond to a competitive situation with more energy than we expend just getting to the stadium. The mystery, of course, is determining just what that optimal level is—I may need a faster heart and breathing rate than you do in order to swim at my best. So for the purposes of prediction we have to study the physiological changes which occur within the particular athlete across several competitive situations. For example, are you more aroused *and* anxious than you were last week under the same conditions? And note that I am saying aroused *and* anxious.

This brings up the third important variable—some athletes are more sensitive than others to arousal and anxiety. I can be aroused and at the same time not be anxious, aware of, and thus distracted by my arousal. My thoughts are on other things rather than on what is going on inside my body. Because I don't recognize the anxiety, I don't try to respond to what is going wrong—for example, increased muscle tension is causing me to miss some easy shots in basketball. At the same time this lack of awareness may also be helpful in that I'm not being distracted by any shortcomings in my performance. In the most simple terms, I just am not worrying about myself and my feelings. Obviously the ideal solution is for the athlete to have an awareness of arousal but to be capable of *not* letting it result in anxiety—in other words, not being distracted by worrisome thoughts and feelings.

Because anxiety can lead to more arousal, and more arousal to even more anxiety, it helps to know as much as possible about the personality and emotional temperament of the individual athlete. Therefore researchers, in addition to concerning themselves with the physiological and subjective aspects of arousal and anxiety, have also recognized the need to study both these areas in terms of *state* and *trait* components.

The trait component refers to the general level of anxiety that you experience across a wide variety of situations—not just on the playing field. Some of us appear more tense and anxious than others, whether we are in practice, studying, or at a party. The higher our general level of tension, the higher our trait for anxiety in all kinds of situations.

By contrast, the state component refers to momentary increases in our level of arousal and anxiety that can be attributed to a particular situation. Since we are concerned here with athletic competition and use the term *arousal* in that context, a perfect example of state anxiety occurs when the athlete moves from practice to game conditions. Obviously, therefore, it's easier to try to lower and control state anxiety than trait anxiety. A person who's always anxious is certainly going to be anxious in a competitive situation, whereas an athlete a bit tense about a big game is only acting like a normal human being.

We will discuss trait and state anxiety later in the book in terms of your self-assessment, but suffice it to say here that any athlete suffering from trait anxiety is having troubles both off, and on, the playing field. And if any athlete's level of anxiety has reached the point, in a particular contest where his performance is actually suffering from it, it's rather academic whether that critical level of anxiety is due to either state and/or trait components)

There has been a tremendous amount of research designed to examine the effects of anxiety on performance. For a long time scientists believed that this relationship could be described as an inverted U. As anxiety first begins to increase, performance improves up to a point, but then, as anxiety continues to increase, performance begins to level off, and with increasing anxiety it begins to deteriorate rapidly. This relationship can be seen in Figure 3.1. Both Western coaches and masters of the martial arts would agree on the viewpoint that presumably the athlete does need to be psyched up, but only to a certain point. To continue to psych him up beyond that point results in dete-

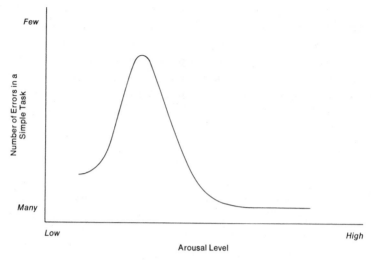

Figure 3.1   Anxiety and Performance

rioration in performance and "choking." However, this parsimonious explanation is both too simple and often incorrect.

More recent research has been carefully controlled and has taken into account the complexity of the performance individuals were asked to engage in under varying levels of anxiety. The results of these studies indicate that the former inverted U conception of the relationship between anxiety and performance is incomplete. What has become apparent is that as anxiety increases, an individual's width of attention narrows.[1] In Chapter 2 it was pointed out that different environmental situations require different widths of attention. The more complex and rapidly changing the competitive situation, the broader your attention must be, but earlier researchers had been asking subjects to perform fairly simple tasks that required narrow attention. Under these conditions increasing anxiety often *did* help the person narrow his attention and thus improve performance. As arousal and anxiety increased even more, attention narrowed too much and performance began to deteriorate. However, if complex tasks had been used, performance would have deteriorated even with small increases in arousal. It almost goes without saying, then, that this relationship between arousal and anxiety, the complexity of the competitive situation, and the width of attention has profound implications for athletic performance.

As it happens, I conducted a study with Robert Walker, a diver on the University of Rochester swim team, and Bill Boomer, the team coach, to examine our divers' ability to perform under different levels of arousal and anxiety. Skin-conductance levels, one measure of arousal, and state anxiety were taken immediately prior to each meet that the University of Rochester divers competed in during the 1975 season. The fluctuations in these measures from meet to meet can be seen as providing an indication of the levels of arousal and anxiety for each diver. It was a simple matter, then, to examine the relationships between the divers' level of arousal and anxiety and their performance on the dives. In addition it was possible to look at the relationship between complexity and performance by noticing which dives were most affected.

The results of this study led to several conclusions: (1) independent of the level of difficulty, the *lower* the level of arousal and the level of anxiety, the *better* the performance; (2) the relationship between the two measures and performance was strongest for the skin-conductance measure. Thus skin conductance was a better predictor of performance when all dives were considered; (3) the complex, optional dives were more affected by increases in arousal and anxiety than the relatively simple required dives; (4) when looking only at performance on the optional dives, there were no differences between the ability of the two measures (arousal and anxiety) to predict performance. Increases in either one resulted in impairment of performance.

Increasing Arousal to Improve Performance

I pointed out earlier that each of us has an optimal level of arousal for a particular competitive situation and that my optimal level may be higher or lower than yours. Speaking in very general terms, I can predict that under most conditions our optimal level of arousal is somewhat *lower* than the level with which we actually enter a situation—that is, most of us have a far greater need to learn to lower arousal than to increase it. This is true even when the task we are confronted with is very simple, such as hitting a baseball.

On the other hand, although research has shown that most of us can broaden and narrow our attention at will *without* being aroused and anxious, there are some individuals who *cannot* narrow attention without being anxious. In the case of athletes these individuals are constantly finding themselves distracted by their own thoughts and by things going on around them. Indeed they might describe themselves as bored with the game. For this type of person, therefore, some increase in physiological arousal may be helpful. There are also occasions when we should be narrowing our attention but are somehow too apathetic to do so. And this is the time when the old locker room speech may be helpful. For example, we might have had a bad first half, and so we go to the locker room feeling beaten. We're feeling something like this: "What a bum day. I can't wait for this game to be over. Here we are losing... and I don't even care." This letdown and internal focus can be overcome in a couple of ways. During half time the coach might give us his patented "win one for the Gipper" speech that he saves for special occasions. This would arouse us and help us develop an external focus that is aimed at winning the game. Of course the important distinction the coach must be able to make in the locker room, before delivering his speech, is whether we are apathetic or anxious. If he gives us the speech when we're anxious instead of apathetic, it only makes us more anxious. Unfortunately the coach cannot always rely on the behavior of the athletes to tell him if they are anxious or apathetic. In both situations athletes often look depressed. They sit slumped over, there's no kidding around, and no one wants to talk. At this time it's important for the coach to know what the athletes are thinking. A tall order, I know, but *not* for the coach who understands the individuals on his team.

Other situations in which arousal may possibly result in improved performance, even for those individuals who can voluntarily narrow attention, include those times when some short, explosive burst of energy is required. The adrenalin flow, provided it does not interfere with mental functioning, can momentarily act to increase the energy and strength an individual has at his disposal. To do this effectively, however, you have to time your arousal so that it coincides with the need for a maximal effort. As an example, a good pole vaulter should not become aroused early in competition because he cannot maintain a sustained level of arousal until the end, particularly if the competition stretches out over a long period of time. The result of early arousal would be clearing fifteen feet as though it were eighteen and missing eighteen when the opportunity to vault at that height finally came.

More is presented later with respect to learning to control high levels of arousal so that they *can* be used to facilitate performance. For the moment, however, it is important to note that there are many more ways anxiety and arousal interfere with performance than ways in which they help. In fact under most circumstances it is better for you to relax. The reasons for the importance of relaxation will become clearer as the ways in which anxiety interferes with performance are discussed in more detail.

As I already mentioned, with increasing anxiety there is a narrowing of attention. Thus the higher the anxiety and the more complex the competitive situation, the more difficulty you have because your narrowing focus does not allow you to react to, much less process, all the important information. Not only do you have difficulty controlling the width of your attention, but as anxiety and fear increase, so does your awareness of the physical symptoms presented in Table 3.1. Of course as muscle tension increases, it begins to interfere with your coordination and timing. Then as heart rate, breathing, perspiration, and blood pressure begin to increase, you become more aware of bodily processes. Suddenly your own physical reactions become distracting and your ability to control the direction of your attention dwindles. You find yourself thinking about your own feelings, and as a consequence, you begin to lose awareness of the competitive situation. By now anxiety as well as arousal has increased. And the more your attention is directed in this fashion, the less capable you are of responding and attending to your opponent. You start making more mistakes; both anxiety and arousal continue to increase; and the loss of control of both your mental and physical functioning goes on in an increasingly destructive spiral.

What happens is that meaningful plays and patterns which develop in athletic situations remain isolated, fragmented events. As a pitcher, for example, you do not notice that a lean by the first-base runner means that he is going to attempt to steal. Since this connection is not made, the runner steals second from you every time he gets on base. In addition instructions from your coach go unheard because your anxiety makes it impossible to focus on them. You are so caught up in your own feelings and thoughts that you don't even notice someone talking to you.

If anxiety from competitive situations continues to increase or remains at a high level for any extended period of time, you experience more dramatic physiological changes. Cramps may develop because of the increased muscle tension, and you must work harder to accomplish the same goal—you have to compensate for tension in muscle groups that is antagonistic to desired performance. This extra work eventually depletes your energy reserves, and fatigue and depression develop. The athlete not only slows down physically, but he makes mental errors.

To take an obvious example, a quarterback needs to be able to maintain a broad attentional focus. Unfortunately, as the competitive situation becomes more stressful to him (e.g., third and long yardage, being behind late in the game), his attention may begin to narrow, making it more difficult to pick up his secondary receivers and the incoming linemen. On a crucial play, the primary receiver is covered and the quarterback, because of narrowed attention, fails to see his secondary receiver, who is wide open. While he's looking for an open receiver, the opposing linemen are looking for him and they locate him before he can throw the ball to anyone. He's thrown for a big loss. Bad enough, but at this point the problem is far from over. Because of the importance of the play and because of his need to be successful—and because anxiety has sharply narrowed his attention—the quarterback can't get his failure out of his mind. He walks to the sidelines, silently cursing himself for his failure. He may even be helped out by the coach and the open receiver, both of whom comment on his ineptness. All this results in additional increases in anxiety, a further narrowing of attention, and a definite increase in the likelihood of similar failure on the next series of downs.

To take another example of a mental error, I know a nationally ranked weight lifter, who, aware of the needs of his event, managed to develop a very narrow attentional focus and also learned to arouse himself in order to get his adrenalin flowing. In practice he lifted about sixty per cent of the weight he hoped to lift in competition. Because he was lifting at partial capacity, he became sloppy about concentrating. He wasn't aware of his failing concentration because at this level of exertion he was physically strong enough to compensate for small mental errors. In competition, however, the weight lifter had to work at full capability and mental errors could not be tolerated.

As it happened, the lifter made it into the finals of a competition, needing to clear and jerk 405 pounds to win. He managed to psych himself up all right, but he wasn't paying proper attention to the job at hand. As he began to yank the bar up from the floor, he was suddenly struck by the thought that it felt like nothing. "It was so easy, I thought I was lifting 250 to 280 pounds," he later told me. This thought, brief though it was, was still enough to cause him to relax his grip and the weights just ripped out of his hands. In effect he attempted to handle 405 pounds in the same way he lifted 280. His narrow focus was directed inappropriately—to the apparent lightness of the weight instead of to the completion of the lift.

These two examples illustrate how anxiety interferes with the cognitive processes of thinking, acquiring knowledge, and reasoning, and leads to mental errors. In acrobatic events such as diving, gymnastics, and some forms of skating, athletes rely a great deal on coordination and timing for successful execution, and increases in arousal resulting in increased muscle tension may disrupt timing and coordination to the extent that the athlete cannot perform. Moreover, in these particular sports, there are many stresses which can increase both the arousal and anxiety levels of a performer. For example, the first attempt of a diver or a gymnast to learn a new movement may be particularly frightening. I can speak with some authority on the matter as I remember vividly what happened the first time I attempted a forward 1½ somersault.

One summer, before my eighth-grade year, I was fortunate enough to be able to get some individual coaching and had managed to develop a few dives. I had been doing a forward somersault for several weeks and, as a result, experienced little anxiety when attempting the dive. I was relaxed and confident in my ability. The coach, noticing the lift I was getting off the board and the speed of my somersault, concluded that if I stayed tucked a little longer, I would be able to execute a 1½ somersault. "That's great," he said, "do a 1½." His words produced a gulp, and as I started thinking about the dive, I also started to get scared. My fear resulted in increasing tension in my neck and shoulder muscles, and this in turn restricted the movement of my head so that I couldn't get my chin down on my chest. Thus I was unable to spin as fast as normal because my ability to spin depended on getting my head down. In addition my anxiety meant that I was pressing—my fears about executing the dive properly plus the belief that I would have to spin faster made me start trying to somersault too soon. In effect I did not wait for the board to lift me into the air. By not waiting, I destroyed the lift of the board and did not get my normal height. The result was that both my normal speed and height were interfered with by my anxiety, and under such conditions I no longer had the ability to do a 1½. Fortunately, I eventually realized what was affecting my performance and in time taught myself to be able to relax when trying new dives. This then allowed me to make fewer painful mistakes and to learn faster.

The preceding examples have focused on either the cognitive or the physical interferences which result from anxiety. Under most competitive conditions, however, disturbances in performance result from both these factors. For example, a tennis player recently came to me because she had been "choking" in competition. In discussing her problems, the following sequence of events became clear. At the start of a match she felt anxious. If by chance she performed well on the first few points, she began to relax and settle down. If she performed poorly, however, several things happened. First her arm, shoulder, and leg muscles began to tense and she found herself stretching to reach for shots instead of taking the time to get set up. The tension increases also made it difficult for her to go low for the ball and to follow through. In addition, her anxiety made her attempt to get set up for a return too soon and she often found herself slightly out of position for the ball. The situation became even more aggravated when she began to talk to herself and punish herself mentally for her mistakes. Her anger resulted in a narrowing of her attention and in an internal focus—she repeatedly thought about earlier lost points instead of concentrating on the ball. This failure to concentrate resulted in still more errors and more frustration. And so on—from a poor start her game deteriorated on an almost predictable basis. I know it sounds like a major task, but actually with a little practice at learning to relax, she was able to overcome this problem. Now when she gets off to a bad start, she doesn't let it ruin her game.

A second and final example involves a college distance swimmer. As with the tennis player, if the swimmer managed to get out to a lead in a hurry or if he knew that he was better than his competition, he was relaxed and swam a good race. However, if he began to concentrate on the competition and started swimming against them instead of swimming his own race, he also began to get anxious. His was almost a classic case. The initial arousal he experienced as a response to the excitement of competition proved to be beneficial if the narrowing of attention happened to result in concentration on his own rhythm and race. However, when his attention became focused on the competition, any movement that looked threatening increased his arousal beyond the point of its being helpful. He then began focusing on his own fears, and his anxiety led to increases in arousal, which in turn increased muscle tension in the neck and shoulders. Inevitably, he had to swim harder and he would tire and tie up, but we gradually got him to swim his own race and let the competition worry about him, instead of vice versa.

In discussing the negative effects of arousal on performance, the focus has been on situations where being psyched up was associated with the flow of adrenalin and the physiological and psychological changes that go along with the release of this chemical into the blood stream. Arousal associated with the physical and cognitive changes presented in Table 3.1 is very different from the excitement and enthusiasm you feel when you have a positive attitude and are looking forward to a competition. Under these conditions your attention is narrowed to constructive positive thoughts which actually prevent you from becoming aroused and fearful. This positive focus results in the tingle that you feel when you know you are ready and expect to win. Interestingly enough, it is precisely this positive excitement which is what coaches call being psyched up and what they assume is associated with the flow of adrenalin and what has been medically called the fight or flight reaction.[2]

At the University of Rochester we measured the level of our swimmers' arousal by measuring their skin conductance just before each meet.[3] For example, with one of our swimmers entered in the 100-yard freestyle in five different meets, I measured his skin conductance at each meet in order to find out how anxious he was. Then, after all five races, I compared his time for the race in which he was least aroused with his average time across the five races or with his time when he was most aroused. What we discovered was that the more aroused the swimmer, the poorer he performed. In fact, if the swim-team members when they were least aroused could actually swim against themselves when they were most aroused, they would cut an average of 3.3 seconds off their times. If a swimmer swam a 54-second 100 with a high level of arousal, he would swim a 50.7-second 100 with a low level. This finding of improved performance was so consistent across swimmers that a dual-meet score would have been 77 to 10—that is, the low-aroused individuals beat themselves by a score of 77 to 10. (The high-aroused team got its ten points for just being in the meet.) More detailed information on this point is presented in the chapter notes.[4]

What is also very interesting about the arousal data we collected is that in those meets where the swimmers were least aroused, the coach thought they were most psyched up. At these meets the team members were talkative and animated, but when arousal, as measured by skin conductance, was high, the swimmers were quiet and kept to themselves. In retrospect, therefore, we learned that when the swimmers were most aroused, they had probably convinced themselves before the meet had ever started that they could not possibly win.

The distinction being made between having a positive, enthusiastic attitude and being physiologically aroused is a vital one. Ironically enough, if the coach *mistakenly* assumes that a positive attitude means adrenalin is flowing and if his attempts at psyching the athlete up result in developing confidence and a positive attitude rather than the flow of adrenalin, he is not differing from the practitioner of the martial arts as far as ultimate goals are concerned. A relaxed athlete is a confident athlete, and the sooner individuals comprehend this, the better they will perform.

Confidence and a positive attitude result in a lowering of anxiety and thus less interference due to antagonistic muscle tension or to a loss of ability to direct and control attention. One method coaches often use to get an athlete to develop confidence is the "power of positive thinking" approach. Stated simply, if you tell yourself you are a winner often enough, you will believe it. For some athletes this seems to be the case, and the coach's saying, "Think like a winner" helps them control attention and arousal and win.

For many others, however, this request is impossible to honor because the thinking isn't being translated into reality. To state the case in the extreme—here I am thirty points behind with a minute left to play and you tell me to convince myself I am a winner. All too often our attempts to tell ourselves we are winners simply force us to look at our failure. The dialogue goes something like this, "Come on, Bob, think like a winner, you're a winner. Oof, what happened? If I'm a winner, what am I doing on the floor?

Come on, get up, try again, you're a winner. Ugh, what's the use? I don't have any wind, it hurts, I'm losing." For some of us it's impossible to convince ourselves mentally—we lose the argument every time. When you feel this way, an Eastern approach may be more helpful.

From an Eastern perspective, an alternate way of ultimately developing confidence and a positive attitude is to become so caught up in things going on outside yourself that you no longer worry about winning or losing. So long as you think about winning or losing instead of attending to the game, you cannot play your best. Those of us who become upset at our failures, who are afraid of losing, become discouraged by our own mistakes and by our opponent's successes. If we can avoid thinking about winning or losing, if we can learn to focus attention *only* on the experience of playing, we can play at a much higher level. This higher level of performance results in our being successful and confidence will develop as a function of our accomplishments. The important point is that many times the only way to reach that ultimate level is to forget about winning or losing *while we are actually playing the game.* And now how many of you are reminded of that old saying—it's not winning or losing but how you play the game that counts!

Thus far, I have been very careful to discriminate between *stress,* which I defined as a situation that had the potential for eliciting arousal (physiological changes), and *anxiety* (psychological worry and fear). Discriminating between these terms is important for two reasons. First, people often use these terms interchangeably, and unless you know that the other person means the same thing you do, it can lead to confusion. For example, I might mention *arousal,* meaning only physiological changes in heart rate or flow of adrenalin, and you may interpret the word as meaning worry and fear. I might then tell you that I believe you are aroused, and because you aren't worried or fearful, you deny it. Obviously this miscommunication becomes critical when a coach and a psychologist argue about the effects of anxiety on performance.

The second reason for discriminating between stress, anxiety, and arousal is because the three do not always go together, and it is very important to be aware of this. Some situations that we might expect to elicit anxiety and arousal do not; thus they are not stressful, even though we think they should be. In addition we don't always respond to stress with increases in both arousal and anxiety. We may experience only changes in heart rate and respiration or we may worry without any physiological changes occurring. It is particularly important to keep these facts in mind when trying to understand or examine any isolated individual situation or example. However, it is less important when talking about anxiety and arousal in general.

Although the individual differences that have been pointed out are real, after examining a large number of situations we find that we can make some valid generalizations. Most often situations we expect to be stressful elicit increases in both anxiety and arousal—the athlete experiences physical changes, and these plus the situation itself generate worry, thereby narrowing attention and destroying concentration. Because arousal and anxiety do go together much of the time, the rest of this book, for ease of reading, uses the terms interchangeably, unless for some reason it is important that reference be made only to the physiological or psychological components of a stress response.

Chapter Four. **Sources of Arousal and Anxiety**

Most sports contain an element of physical danger, but surprisingly, anxiety created by a physical threat often impairs performance less than the anxiety caused by emotional turmoil. There are two reasons for this. First, it's much easier for us to identify physical threats than emotional ones. As a result physical threats have a more limited effect on our functioning.

For instance, you may have successfully executed one particular dive so many times that anxiety is no longer associated with it. Then you begin to learn another dive, and occasional mistakes occur. Since these mistakes are upsetting, a certain amount of physical fear is still associated with each attempt of the new dive.

Compare the effects of anxiety under the conditions just described with the effects of anxiety that occur as a function of a more general emotional fear, the fear of failure. Such a fear affects every aspect of the competitive situation because our performance is under constant observation and evaluation, both by ourselves and by others. Thus our arousal level is increased to a degree on all the dives, not just on the ones we are unsure of performing well.

The other factor in coping with physical threats concerns our ability to accept the anxious feelings that develop. Most of us are capable of accepting and admitting to a "healthy fear"—that is, it is socially appropriate for us to be afraid of breaking our necks. In fact we may even feel better about ourselves for recognizing a certain amount of fear when that fear is associated with the threat of actual injury. In effect our accomplishment seems greater and our acceptance of the fear frees us to think of other things. We don't have to invest energy in convincing ourselves that we are not afraid. Instead we respond by recognizing the fear, telling ourselves, "That's all right, that's the way I should feel," and redirecting our attention externally to the task at hand.

I remember a personal experience that illustrates the role of fear all too well. In high school a friend and I took two girls swimming one afternoon. We went to a very fancy place that had an Olympic-size pool complete with a ten-meter (thirty-five-foot) tower. Neither my friend nor I had ever seen anything higher than a three-meter diving board. While the girls walked off to get something to eat, we decided to climb up on the tower and take a look. We were up there admiring the view and thinking how stupid someone would have to be to dive off anything that high when the girls came back looking for us. They looked around the pool, didn't see us, and then started to look elsewhere. We yelled to let them know where we were and to tell them that we were coming down. They looked up, saw us, and my date, brave girl, yelled, "Dive!"

The proverbial lump stuck in my throat; suddenly I realized how high up we were. My fear made the girls seem smaller and the pool seem even further down. As I stood there panic-stricken, my friend strolled over to the edge and looked down. Then he straightened up, thumbed his nose at the girls, turned, and climbed back down the same way we had come up. I knew that if I walked over to the edge and looked down before attempting to dive, I wouldn't attempt the dive. I also knew that if I was going to try it, I should dive out since I would probably flip over onto my back if I dove straight down.

With the girls and my friend looking up, I took a deep breath, ran towards the edge of the tower, and without looking, launched myself into the air. I assumed a position that roughly resembled a swan dive with my arms extended out to the side. I was so frightened that my attention narrowed and I lost awareness of everything. Just before I hit the water, I remember thinking, "My God, Bob, your hands are still out at your sides." I had been so frightened that I had forgotten to bring my hands back over my head to enter the water. I made a desperate attempt just before hitting and got them over my head but not quite together. I hit the water, and it felt as if someone tried to jerk both arms out of their sockets. The impact caused me to somersault, and I'm sure that I didn't go more than three feet under the water.

When I climbed out of the pool, I had a sore back and the admiration of both girls. And despite my stinging back, I felt pleased with myself. In spite of my fear, which was natural given the danger (as painfully demonstrated by how I hit the water), I had tried. I felt so good, in fact, that I went back up on the tower and did it right.

As I mentioned above, it's harder for us to deal with our emotional fears. Many athletes are particularly hesitant to admit they fear failure. They feel the mere admission implies a large—if not total—lack of self-confidence, and they believe that such an admission is bad. And of course inability to accept these emotional fears results in a very destructive influence on our performance.

I remember hearing a professional football coach tell his team that "any athlete who talks about being afraid or

thinks of losing has a bad attitude and is already a loser."
This kind of statement makes it almost impossible for a
player who *is* frightened of losing to resolve the problem
effectively. I can speak of this with some authority because
in high school I had a football coach who said the same
thing to me, and I remember the conflict it produced.
Being a teenager, I believed the coach, and because I was
sometimes frightened, I thought something was wrong
with me. I often found myself spending more time trying to
talk myself out of feeling a certain way than I spent concentrating on the game. The result was that I made even more
mistakes because I was distracted, and my self-esteem
drifted even lower.

The need for self-esteem is an almost universal char-
acteristic—we all have a strong desire to feel good about
ourselves. In fact one of the major reasons for engaging
in competitive athletics is the potential for developing
self-esteem. When we are first competing in a particular
sport, various problems develop because we lack the experience to evaluate our own performance. Having little
choice in the matter, we rely on the feelings and reactions
others give us to obtain the self-esteem we desire. Our
self-esteem at this point is highly dependent upon external
cues—having a better time or distance than our opponent
or getting a positive response from the crowd or our teammates. Since lack of experience makes it difficult for us to
predict how well we will perform in a particular situation,
this lack of belief in ourselves can lead to anxiety. At this
point in our development we are competing against others
rather than against ourselves, and it's possible for us to
perform horribly yet feel good because we won.

In looking to others for confirmation of success or failure,
we are allowing ourselves to be dominated by an external
attentional focus, and we will be overly responsive to en-

vironmental cues. A face made by our coach can be devastating. Antics by an opponent may cause us to "choke." When these go on early in the contest, we become distracted and see only failure ahead. Instead of concentrating on playing as well as we can, we respond by becoming anxious and tensing up. We've beaten ourselves.

Naturally enough, as our experience increases, we become more capable of predicting the outcome of a particular competition and we begin to develop our own internal norms for personal success and failure. This experience allows a Walt Frazier or a Fran Tarkenton to say, "I'm a pro, I know what I can do, and I don't get psyched out by an opponent's games." Because these athletes have experienced a wide range of competitive situations and have faced a variety of opponents, they have an accurate picture of their own strengths and weaknesses. The clearer their understanding of their abilities, the less their performance is affected by the isolated and often fickle responses of crowds—and coaches.

As an athlete's experience grows, he begins to know his capabilities and thus develops a more consistent level of performance. If this level is higher than most of the competition, then some important emotional changes take place. External reinforcements such as trophies and ribbons begin to lose their meaning after they become commonplace. Winning and the appreciation of the coach and crowd are no longer so exciting. At this point one of two things must occur if we are to be able to maintain our involvement in the sport. Either we must move up to a higher level of competition, where there is danger of the whole process I have just described repeating itself, or we must direct our attention internally and begin competing with ourselves.

The tendency to begin competing against ourselves has some obvious advantages. We'll be much less likely to "choke" because of the performance of our competitors. If we're running the mile at our own pace, the introduction of a "rabbit" into the race (to set the pace) doesn't upset us. Our own goals have been set in advance and we know how to perform independently of the other competitors. In addition, as we begin to compete against ourselves it becomes easier to remain motivated and to continue to practice without external competition.

At this stage in development, there is a shift with respect to what causes our anxiety because as we become more seasoned, anxiety gets generated by our own expectancies and demands rather than by environmental factors. By and large the primary source for much of this anxiety is the setting of unrealistic goals. For one thing, as we begin competing against ourselves, we may begin to lose sight of our physical and emotional limitations. We may also forget that some luck is involved in performance. If we have had one truly exceptional day, we automatically raise our standards and expect, even demand, of ourselves that every day be like that "finest hour." Once a person has broken 70 on the golf course, rolled a perfect game in bowling, or run the mile in under four minutes, it's difficult to be satisfied with less. These unreasonable expectations can create major problems.

This is not to say that an athlete should not try to reach this new plateau of performance on a consistent basis, but it may not be possible at this stage of development, and his expectations are unreasonable rather than realistic. Even a seasoned athlete can "choke," especially when he loses to himself. The interior dialogue that this produces is all too familiar, but because of its importance it bears repeating: "Damn it, how could you have missed that shot, you've made it a hundred times! What's the matter with you, you're playing like a five-year-old! Concentrate, damn it, concentrate! If you can't play better than this you deserve to lose. Here it comes, get ready, now get down on the ball, get down on the ball, don't chop at this one."

This inner dialogue goes on in a variety of forms—some of us use much more explicit language—and in all sports. Again, it only serves to distract the athlete, to keep him from flowing with the game. As a result the athlete makes an increasing number of errors and he experiences a decrease in the joy that should be associated with the sport. What's ironic in this instance is that behind the implicit assumption which sometimes forces a fine athlete to be dissatisfied with less than perfection is the belief that unless he strives for perfection, he won't improve. Unfortunately the reality is that unless an athlete can set realistic goals and emotionally accept less than perfection, he won't ever attain his ultimate potential.

Obviously enough, the less proficient you feel you are, the more conscious the thought which goes into your play, whether in practice or in competition. However, to the extent that conscious effort can be valuable to you, it should be limited as much as possible to practice. Quite simply, the more you have to think about what you're doing, the more likely it is that you won't respond appropriately to your opponent. But note that the emphasis here is not placed on a complete avoidance of being dissatisfied with progress and development. Be dissatisfied, but be dissatisfied at the right time—in *practice*—not in the game. Ideally, under competitive circumstances you do not think about your next move—it's so familiar to you that it's performed automatically.

We've been speaking about anxiety in competitive situations and how the athlete generates much of this anxiety. Still, let's not ignore the opponent who's going to probe for your emotional weaknesses—just as you're going to probe for his—and let's not ignore your much more unfortunate, unintentional sources of anxiety, be they your friends, your parents, or even your coaches.

As anyone who has ever attended a Little League baseball game or a Pop Warner football contest can attest, the parents in the stands and on the sidelines are both the players' most ardent fans and most vociferous critics. The pressure which parents sometimes put on their offspring to excel in athletics is most unhealthy—after all, in all forms of competition someone has to lose or come in last. Then, too, parents as well as coaches do a swell job of interfering with the players' performance by reminding them of their shortcomings at precisely the wrong time. They lose patience, clutch their foreheads, and grimace as the players make a mistake. Or they smile in a condescending way and say, "It's all right, I know you can do better." Using their own brand of parlor psychology, they may tell the players to "be confident, you can do it." The net effect of all this emphasizes that their children are not making it on their own. Consider how Gordie Howe's son, Mark, must have felt when he and his famous father were first out there on the ice together, and the fans taunted, "That's it, Daddy, tell little Markie where to go."

I have a classic example of how anxiety can get blown out of proportion and even end an athlete's career because well-meaning people are often completely insensitive to what the athlete is feeling. And sadly, there are literally thousands of stories like this one. Early in the 1974 basketball season I had a varsity forward come into my office. He told me that he was unsure about his position on the team—he wasn't getting along with the coach and he was feeling a tremendous amount of pressure. He was worried about looking good in comparison to the talented, ambitious freshmen and sophomores on the team. He was also worried about assuming a role of leadership. All the anxiety and arousal had made him so tense that he wasn't able to get full extension of his arms when rebounding or driving for a layup. When he was out on the court, he was so tight that his shoulders looked like Ed Sullivan's.

By the time he came in to see me, all his confidence in his own ability was gone and his performance had gotten progressively poorer. He was making seventh-grade mistakes, missing layups, failing to rebound, and not taking wide-open shots. The coach was on the player's back and had moved him down from the number-four spot to the number-eleven spot on the squad. In addition to all his other woes, the player was having a recurrent nightmare. In this dream he found himself standing beside a table. Erected in the middle of the table at about shoulder height was a basket. He reached out and tried to drop a ball through the basket only to find that the basket had moved. Each time he tried to make the basket he failed and woke up in frustration, feeling like a failure.

Although this athlete could not speak openly with his coach, he did share his concerns not only with me but also with some of the older players—who were as supportive as they could be. I designed a program to teach him to relax and to help him overcome his fear of missing shots. We worked on the program for six weeks and we were making progress. He was feeling more confident, but unfortunately now he wasn't getting into the games, so he was unable to show the coach what he could do.

At last, toward the end of the first half of a very close game, the coach told him to go in. After running up and down the court a couple of times, a teammate passed off to him on a fast break. He got the ball, drove for the layup, and made it despite one of the opposing players hanging all over him. He was delirious with joy and so were his teammates. Three of them ran up to him shouting, slapping his palms in the congratulatory gesture all athletes use these days, almost as excited for him and his personal victory as he was himself. He went to the line and made the foul shot, completing the three-point play. Incredibly, the coach sent in a substitute for him. As he walked past the coach, he wasn't even noticed—the coach was too busy yelling instructions to the guy going into the game.

The coach was another victim of his own anxiety. His own concerns kept him from being aware of his players and of their needs. His insensitivity at a time when his support was most needed resulted in this athlete again losing confidence and eventually quitting basketball.

Social Learning

As I mentioned before, while parents and teammates may be unaware of the effect they may have on your behavior, opponents are acutely aware. When an athlete is successful in psyching you out, he's caused you to lose control over your attentional processes, to focus on the wrong things. As usual this inappropriate focus leads to mistakes, which in turn result in increasing tension and arousal.

At a swim meet, two swimmers were standing on the starting blocks. The starter called them to their marks. One of the individuals intentionally false-started. He dove in, swam underwater into his opponent's lane, and then slowly swam back down the lane to the end of the pool. As he climbed out next to his competitor and walked past, he whispered, "I just pissed in your lane." The next time the starter called them to their marks, his competitor had difficulty directing attention to the starter's commands. As the gun went off, he got a slow start because he was thinking of diving into a puddle of urine instead of into the water.

Most of us are raised in ways which cause us to develop

attitudes and values that can interfere with our ability to perform. We develop a self-concept that says we should respect other people, play fair, never hit a person when he is down, and so forth. These ingrained social responsibilities are often used by our opponents to psych us out.

For instance, some boxers, among them Muhammad Ali, exaggerate the effects of an opponent's blow in an attempt to get him to let up. They rely on the fact that most people are reluctant to hit a man when he's down. If an opponent lacks the "killer" instinct, the tactic works.

The extent to which our moral and social values influence or inhibit performance is much broader than many people believe. I remember playing in a mixed-sex tackle football game and rolling on the ground, laughing at the inhibition of one of my friends. He happened to be playing defensive end, and a particularly busty girl came running towards him with the ball. He braced himself, raised his arms and hands, and prepared to tackle her around the shoulders. A look of surprise came over him as he realized he had his hands out as if to grab her chest. He moved his hands and eyes down, getting ready to hit her low, and found himself staring at—and reaching towards—her pelvic area. He shifted between these two points about three times and then stood flat-footed as she ran right past him for a touchdown.

Who's Ugliest?

Boxers often play a psyching game with each other called *Who's ugliest?* Sonny Liston gave us perhaps the most famous example of a cold, hard stare; George Foreman also uses it. The idea behind the move is to impress upon the opponent that you have no love for him, that you are *real* mean, and that if it's possible, you'll destroy him. Another tactic is to refuse to shake hands. Still another is spitting at the floor in disgust as a form of greeting. Football players make it a point to hit their opposition as though they are mortal enemies; in this way they give the opposition something to think about the next time they come that way. Insults are traded, and as a player gets up from a pile, he may consciously shove another player's head into the ground. Running backs who get hit hard bounce up after they have been really clobbered to keep the tackler from knowing that they are hurt. It's all the psyching game. Bill Russell once revealed how he was able to intimidate offensive players. He made sure that the first few times he went up to block a shot, he did just that. Having established an area around the basket as his territory, he made opposing players wary of even being in the neighborhood. They changed the normal arc of their shot to avoid being stuffed, and more often than not they missed the basket.

It's in the Bag

There are more subtle ways of intimidating opponents in noncontact sports. A favorite trick of many athletes is to appear very self-confident. Pole vaulters and high jumpers skip lower heights. Some divers place their best dive first in an attempt to impress both the judges and their competition. They know that a "halo effect" can develop and that the judge is likely to score them higher on subsequent dives as a function of that first impression. And that good first dive puts more pressure on the competition.

Other athletes are masters at appearing cool and unruffled by events going on around them. They act relaxed and nonchalant and may not even appear concerned enough to warm up. They leave their sweat suits on for an extra long time or take a nap. This apparent calm often reminds an opponent of his anxiety and causes him to worry more. "He seems so relaxed," the opponent worries. "What's the matter with *me?*"

Side Comments

There is another group of athletes who drop little side comments designed to be overheard by their competitors. They talk to a teammate, close enough so the competition can overhear, and say something like, "Oh, I'm not worried about this meet, I'm pointing to the nationals," or, "I'm really up for today—I feel ready to run a 4:03 mile." Inevitably the time is calculated to at least ten seconds better than their opponent's best previous efforts. Most of these tactics have their greatest effect on less experienced athletes. The more experienced individuals know what to believe and what not to believe. Generally they don't pay any attention to the remarks and aren't even aware of their opponents' attempts to psych them out.

The anxiety which athletes experience is by no means limited to the competitive situation. The last ten years in our history have seen political pressure groups including the AAU and NCAA trying to dictate when and how athletes will compete. When slugger Hank Aaron was rewriting the baseball record book, he was subjected to threats on his life if he broke Babe Ruth's record. More recently, in the 1975 World Series, an umpire received threats to his family because of a controversial call he made. There are a multitude of social, religious, and moral factors that can serve to interfere with athletic performance. In each instance the athlete's attention is drawn away from the competitive situation toward some irrelevant fear, concern, or object. A runner gets a poor start in a hundred-yard dash because he is thinking about a very close relative who is very ill. An outfielder fails to catch up with a long fly ball because he has been thinking about the slambang argument he had with his wife. There are uncountable thousands of these potential sources of anxiety and it is of course impossible to deal with them all successfully. What this complex situation highlights is the fact that an athlete must gain control over his attentional processes if he wishes to perform at his best.

I mentioned there are occasions when it might be worthwhile to arouse an athlete so that the adrenalin flows, but such instances are rare. The major reason would be to take advantage of the concomitant increases in strength that coincide with it. Under certain circumstances this increase in strength might be used effectively by the athlete, but there are several factors militating against this. First, the arousal would have to occur at a precise moment in competition. Second, the situation would have to be a very stable one where a simple automatic chain of responses is all that is required of the athlete—as, say, in weight lifting. Finally, the increased muscle tension associated with the arousal would have to be specific and nonantagonistic to those muscle groups where increases aid performance, and given a high level of arousal, this is very unlikely. All these factors require that the athlete's arousal be under an internal focus of control—that is, he deliberately psychs himself up—rather than an external or environmental one.

Most of us can rarely use this increased flow of adrenalin. This is especially true in team sports, when we are expected to be able to respond to each movement of our opponents in head-to-head competition. Arousal here would be like going rabbit hunting with a cannon—seldom do we need that kind of firepower. In fact we really shouldn't rely that much on strength, especially when that strength is associated with a loss of control over attentional processes.

The stories of superstrength resulting from arousal fail to point out that while a woman was carrying a 300-pound stove out of her burning house, she was forgetting about her children. In a similar way the football guard hyped up on an adrenalin flow charges through a mass of blockers, then tackles the running back on one play, looking like the village idiot when his opponents run a trap up the middle. If he happens to recover a fumble and be facing the wrong way, he runs eighty yards and scores a touchdown—for the other team. Or he's called for roughing the passer or for unsportsmanlike conduct because he continues to charge after the play is over. Once set in motion, he just *goes*—his body is working, but not his brain.

A perfect example of this kind of behavior took place during the first half of the 1975–76 professional basketball season. During a National Basketball Association game between the Buffalo Braves and the Milwaukee Bucks, Dick Gibbs of the Braves and Gary Brokaw of the Bucks got into some physical contact which isn't part of the game. The scuffle grew into a fracas, with the Bucks' tall forward, Bob Dandridge, tackling Brokaw, and a game of football might have ensued (without any football) if calmer minds hadn't prevailed. (The cause of order was greatly facilitated by the peace-keeping efforts of one king-sized peace-keeper, six-foot-eight, 280-pound Wayne Embry, a former player who is now general manager of the Bucks.) After the game, when Gibbs was questioned about a bruise on one of his knuckles, he admitted. "Yeah, I hit somebody. I was waiting to be ejected. I should have been. You know, you play with intensity, and when you do that, tempers flare up. I was coming in off the bench and I was frustrated. I might have a tendency to take it out on somebody." In this case, you'll agree, playing with intensity was no substitute for playing with intelligence.

Accordingly, if you hope to be in control of yourself during athletic competition and want to maximize your potential, you *must* learn to relax in order to reach that point when you know both *when* and *how* to arouse yourself. Just as someone attempting to learn to drive doesn't do so with the throttle shoved to the floor, neither should you expect to learn with the adrenalin flowing.

A few years ago it was easier for coaches of professional athletes to rely on external controls to keep an athlete's attention focused and under control. Rules were set which kept environmental distractions to a minimum. For example, spouses could not travel with the team. Reporters, scouts, and recruiters were kept out of the locker room and away from players. The choice of people allowed to fraternize with the athletes was dictated by the coaching staff. Training tables were set up so that all meals would be eaten together. Curfews were established, as well as regulations against smoking, drinking, and later on, modes of dress and length of hair. Workouts were usually strenuous enough to keep athletes too tired to break regulations or to think about distractions.

The ability of professional teams to maintain an isolated existence was much easier in the past, but now the attitudes of the public—and the athletes themselves—have changed. We see ABC-TV announcers talking to divers just before they dive off a hundred-foot tower in a high wind. The President of the United States calls pro football coaches in their locker rooms and suggests plays before crucial games. Everyone from the team owner to the kid peeking through a knothole wants a part of the action. The result of all this is that external control over potential distraction is almost impossible to maintain. Coaches can no longer expect to be in control of their athletes' psyches.

Athletics has expanded and grown more impersonal, and coaches now have large staffs of assistants to handle all phases of the game. The head coach, except at very small high schools and colleges, is too busy recruiting players and then training them, to spend time with individual athletes—the exceptions, of course, being the stars of the team who will help make the coach's reputation. As his contact with each player becomes more limited, the coach obviously loses his ability to act as any kind of personal counselor. In truth he has neither the time nor the motivation to do so, and perhaps inadvertently he becomes one of the key adults forcing the young athlete to "cut the apron strings" and "grow up." Not only is this sad in a sense, but it is also wrong in terms of good coaching—the successful coach of the future will be the one who is able to facilitate—not ignore—the personal growth of the athlete, while he, the coach, coordinates the activities of a large staff.

With or without—but hopefully *with*—a coach's help, the athlete of today must learn to gain control over both physiological and psychological processes. As noted and emphasized earlier, the key to all this is to learn to relax and then to learn how and where to direct attentional processes. Only this control allows the athlete to think about personal problems under appropriate circumstances—in other words, where they do not interfere with performance. Attentional control is the psychological/emotional element needed to integrate ability and performance, and more important still, it ultimately allows the individual to function more effectively in virtually every aspect of his life.

Chapter Five. **Self-Assessment**

This chapter shows you how to assess your own level of anxiety and your attentional style. To be able to predict your own success or failure within a particular competitive situation, you must know what the attentional demands of the sport are—for example, does it usually demand a narrow-external focus?—what your own attentional capabilities are, and how much your abilities are likely to be modified by the arousal you experience in the competitive situation. By isolating those factors that affect the type of attentional focus you need in competition as well as by identifying the factors which cause you to become anxious, you automatically gain some control over your behavior. For instance, if you become distracted by external stimuli, you can work on reducing them or tuning them out.

The Assessment of Anxiety

There has been a great deal of research activity designed to examine how different individuals experience anxiety and respond to stressful situations. Researchers have studied the subjective statements of people about how anxious they feel. They have examined the subjects' anxious behavior patterns—for example, how many cigarettes they smoke, how much their hands shake, if they bite their nails. In addition they have analyzed such physiological measures of arousal as changes in skin-conductance levels (amount of perspiration), in muscle tension (electromyograph—EMG), in heart rate, in respiration rate, and in brain wave activity (electroencephalogram—EEG). All this research activity taken together has led to the discovery of several important factors which affect an individual's anxiety level.

State and Trait Anxiety

When talking about your level of anxiety and arousal, we can, as noted earlier, talk about it in terms of both state and trait components. Naturally each of us has a certain base level of anxiety that we carry around with us all the time. Otherwise we'd be robots. As you know, this is the trait component, and presumably individuals who are described as chronically anxious or nervous would score high on any test designed to measure this trait. In addition to the trait component, we tend to respond by increasing our base level of arousal and anxiety in stressful situations. Increases in response to changing situations are the state components of anxiety. As I've said, generally speaking it's easier to learn to modify and control state anxiety than trait anxiety. So when you are assessing your own level of anxiety, it's important to discriminate between the two. To do this, you need to obtain and compare measures of your arousal and anxiety (e.g., your subjective feelings, physiological measures such as skin conductance, respiration, etc.) under a variety of competitive situations.

Individual Differences

We all differ with respect to how we respond to tension. Some of us get increased muscle tension in our necks and shoulders, others in our backs or legs. That's fairly common. A more unusual response is feeling nauseous on a full stomach. Other individuals experience dizziness or heart palpitations. Still others become so defensive that they react to stressful situations by becoming lethargic and falling asleep. Such vastly different responses to stress create special problems for the coach. As a result different approaches must be used for different athletes, and athletes, coaches, and psychologists must not rely on a single kind of behavior as an indication of anxiety.

It becomes critical, therefore, to assess the basic attentional and physical skills required for a certain level of performance and then to relate this to the athlete. Does his response (physiologically *and* psychologically) to stress interfere with his ability to meet performance demands? For example, increased muscle tension in the neck and shoulders would interfere with his ability to catch a pass. He would be unable to get maximum extension of his arms and would not reach passes that he might reach under less stressful circumstances. Some athletes appear to be able to adapt so that the anxiety they experience remains in an area which does not affect their performance. A wide receiver for the Buffalo Bills told me he never experienced tension in his arms or legs. Instead all his anxiety centered in his stomach. Although he would just as soon have avoided the experience of anxiety altogether, at least it did not interfere with his pass-catching ability.

Awareness of Tension

How you experience anxiety in a stressful situation dictates how you go about controlling it. Thus your ability to perceive tension—to feel the arousal which is present—is very important. A well-known tennis player once asked me a number of questions about how anxiety interferes with performance. I described how attention was affected by anxiety and how muscles tense as you become aroused. I went on to explain how this tension disturbs the rhythm of the game and the timing of shots. He responded by saying that he didn't experience the anxiety I was talking about, yet on some days his performance was terrible. In effect he was telling me that he was unable to detect his own feelings of tension and that they did not seem to be tied to a particular level of competition or, for that matter, to feelings of failure. For this man, anxiety (or as he described it, poor performance) could as easily appear in practice as in a high level of competition. Because worry was not always associated with tension, he did not relate his poor playing to increased anxiety and muscle tension. The point here is that although high-level competition often increases anxiety, this is not always the case and should not be used as the model of stress for every athlete. With this particular athlete we had to look at his stress responses independent of a particular level of competition and independent of any sense on his part of having experienced anxiety and/or tension.

Without watching him play, I began to describe to him what his shots were like on his bad days. I told him to think about his shots on these occasions and he would probably notice that when he was playing poorly, he was hitting the ball near the wood at the top of the racquet, either above or below the center line. He was amazed. That was precisely his problem, he said. Now I helped him to understand how increased muscle tension was keeping him from getting to balls that he normally reached. And these restrictions in movement meant that he couldn't get in position to hit the ball in the center of the racquet.

Lacking awareness of increasing tension, the athlete finds it very difficult to perform consistently. Obviously it's impossible to make adjustments for tension changes if you aren't aware of the tension in the first place. In addition, once you finally become aware of the tension in a particular competitive situation, it's usually too late to do anything about it. By this time it has probably increased to the point that it's out of your control.

Too often we attribute mistakes to faulty technique rather than to anxiety. When this occurs in baseball, for instance, we compensate for errors by changing our stance at the plate or our grip on the bat. This may work for a short period of time, but as anxiety decreases, our corrections become overcorrections and suddenly we find ourselves ahead of the pitch. In golf we find ourselves burying the head of the club in the ground behind the ball or hooking it. The distortions in performance that these overcorrections can produce may result in severe damage to an athlete's self-confidence in a particular situation and on occasion in permanent impairment to performance.

There are some classic examples of the downward spiral in performance and the jumping from technique to technique. Wilt Chamberlain has to be one of the most famous examples. Throughout his career, but most markedly toward the end, Wilt was practically notorious for his ineptitude at the foul line. This drew particular attention because Wilt's role with the Los Angeles Lakers changed from the role he had with the Philadelphia 76ers. He wasn't expected to lead the league in scoring but rather to "feed" Jerry West and Gail Goodrich. Still and all, when he did go to the foul line—which he did quite often, because opponents deliberately fouled Chamberlain rather than risk a basket in a tight game—it was usually a one-point play at best. Wilt shot fouls just fine in practice but barely made half his attempts in actual competition. In fact during the 1972–73 season, when Wilt led the league in field-goal accuracy with seventy-three per cent, he shot fifty-one per cent at the foul line.

How does one explain this disparity in skills? In one game in 1962, when Wilt scored the all-time pro basketball high of 100 points in a game against the New York Knicks, he hit twenty-eight of thirty-two shots from the foul line. Yet his career average for foul-shooting was in the low fifty per cent bracket. The fans, the living room coaches, and Wilt's own teammates all had explanations for Wilt's troubles at the foul line. One of the more popular theories was that Wilt was too strong to shoot fouls accurately, but then wouldn't that same strength be a hindrance in making baskets, particularly for a center who worked close to the basket? No, Wilt obviously experienced anxiety—from past poor performances—and increased tension at the foul line. So he tried a never-ending chain of techniques to overcome the problem. He shifted to different places on the foul line—and behind the foul line. One week he was off to the left, the next week he was clear at the back of the key. He tried one-hand shots, he tried shooting underhanded. He even tried psychoanalysis. Wilt's experiences at the foul line and then his attempt at the psychoanalysis of his problem are especially interesting because they illustrate a major mistake concerning such attempts to help athletes overcome anxiety-related problems.

There are two basic problems here—time and technique. The analyst attempts to understand the basic anxieties and subconscious fears of his patient—and make him more aware of his problems. Since treatment is a long-term process, and major personality changes are expected, this sensitization and increased knowledge of anxiety are important. However, in the majority of athletic situations, this approach proves more destructive than constructive. Sensitization worsens performance and increases the downward spiral and feelings of failure and frustration. Instead attention must be redirected *away* from the worries and fears, and the athlete must learn to relax.

It would be wonderful to report otherwise, but the detection of increases and decreases in anxiety is not always an easy process. Therefore Table 5.1 presents a general checklist that you can use to begin determining how you are physiologically affected by stress. To fill out the table, compare your performance on two different occasions. Pick an instance in which you performed well and one in which you performed poorly, and then check off those functions that seemed to be affected under each condition.

The particular pattern of your responses on the anxiety checklist will be useful later in determining just what types of psychological procedures will be helpful to you. However, in addition to assessing your level of arousal, it is just as important to assess your attentional capabilities. Specific information about how arousal affects your attention and how this in turn affects your performance must be available in order to understand past successes and failures. As your attentional strengths and weaknesses and their interactions with anxiety become defined, it's possible to predict in advance how well you will perform in various situations. At

Table 5.1   Anxiety Checklist

	Playing Poorly	Playing Well
Muscle Tension Increases		
1. Right side of neck and shoulder	____	____
2. Left side of neck and shoulder	____	____
3. Chest muscle tension	____	____
4. Tension in right calf muscle	____	____
5. Tension in left calf muscle	____	____
6. Tension headache	____	____
7. Tension in the lower back	____	____
8. Stomach cramps	____	____
9. Fatigue in right arm	____	____
10. Fatigue in left arm	____	____
General Feelings		
1. Feeling light-headed and dizzy	____	____
2. Feeling unsteady as though out of position	____	____
3. Increased perspiration on hands and fingers	____	____
4. Feeling of nausea	____	____
5. Increased heart rate and respiration	____	____
Performance Skills		
1. Unable to cover as much area	____	____
2. Movements choppy	____	____
3. Failure to follow through	____	____
4. Reaction time slowed	____	____
5. Endurance level reduced	____	____
Mental Processes		
1. Talk to self in a negative way ("idiot")	____	____
2. Focus attention on mistakes	____	____
3. Argue with self about how to concentrate	____	____
4. Become angry	____	____
5. Become caught in own thoughts and lose awareness of what's going on around you	____	____
6. Begin warning yourself about mistakes to watch out for ("don't hook")	____	____
7. Attention to things going on around you becomes restricted to one or two things.	____	____

the same time this knowledge can be used to select procedures for improving your control over your level of arousal
and your attention to competition.

Testing Your Attentional Style

For me to be able to predict how you will perform in a
competitive situation, I must first know if you can develop
the type of attention required *under nonstress conditions*
(relaxed practice sessions). Can you broaden and narrow
attention and can you direct it internally and externally?
Next I need to know how you react physically and atten-
tionally under conditions of stress. Finally I need to know if
you are capable of shifting from one focus to another
whenever you want to.

At the University of Rochester we have been developing
a paper and pencil test that attempts to provide us with this
information. By your answering a number of questions
about how you have functioned in the past, it's possible for
us to conclude to some degree of accuracy what your attentional strengths and weaknesses are. For example, if you
say that it's easy for you to shut out everything and concentrate on a book, you're telling me that you can effectively
narrow your attention. If, on a question about athletics, you
indicate that you make mistakes because you concentrate
on one player and forget about what other players are doing, I know that you can narrow attention, but you are
unable to broaden it, and when a broad focus is demanded,
you have difficulty. With this kind of information, plus
additional knowledge about your level of anxiety, I can
suggest procedures for you to use to learn to broaden your
attention.

One simple way for you to begin to learn about your
attentional processes is to answer the questions in Table

Table 5.2 Attentional Assessment

Never
Rarely
Sometimes
Frequently
All the time

BET (Broad-External)

1. I am good at quickly analyzing a complex situation such as how a play is developing in football or which of four or five kids started a fight. _____
2. In a room filled with children or on a playing field I know what everyone is doing. _____

BET Total _____

OET (External Overload)

1. When people talk to me, I find myself distracted by the sights and sounds around me. _____
2. I get confused trying to watch activities such as a football game or circus where many things are happening at the same time. _____

OET Total _____

BIT (Broad-Internal)

1. All I need is a little information and I can come up with a large number of ideas. _____
2. It is easy for me to bring together ideas from a number of different areas. _____

BIT Total _____

OIT (Internal Overload)

1. When people talk to me, I find myself distracted by my own thoughts and ideas. _____
2. I have so many things on my mind that I become confused and forgetful. _____

OIT Total _____

NAR (Narrow Effective Focus)

1. It is easy for me to keep thoughts from interfering with something I am watching or listening to. _____
2. It is easy for me to keep sights and sounds from interfering with my thoughts. _____

NAR Total _____

RED (Errors of Underinclusion)

1. I have difficulty clearing my mind of a single thought or idea. _____
2. In games I make mistakes because I am watching what one person does and I forget about the others. _____

RED Total _____

5.2. After you've finished with the questions, total up your answers by assigning a value from 0 to 4 to each response, as indicated below. Next total your score for each of the two-item subscales (e.g., BET, OET, OIT) and then plot them on Figure 5.1.

$$0 = \text{Never}$$
$$1 = \text{Rarely}$$
$$2 = \text{Sometimes}$$
$$3 = \text{Frequently}$$
$$4 = \text{All the time}$$

Table 5.3 presents a brief definition of each of the attentional subscales. Don't become too concerned with the high or low position of your score on a particular scale. Since individuals perceive themselves and their worlds differently, it makes little sense to compare your scores with

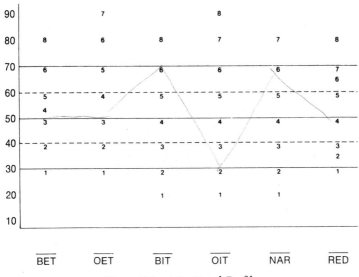

Figure 5.1 Attentional Profile

Table 5.3   Attentional Subscale Definitions

BET (Broad-External)

The higher the score, the more the individual's answers indicate that he deals effectively with a large number of external stimuli. He has a broad-external focus that is effective.

OET (External Overload)

The higher the score, the more the individual's answers indicate that he makes mistakes because he is overloaded and distracted by external stimuli. He has difficulty narrowing attention when he needs to.

BIT (Broad-Internal)

The higher the score, the more the individual indicates that he is able to think about several things at once when it is appropriate to do so. He has a broad-internal focus.

OIT (Internal Overload)

The higher the score, the more the individual indicates that he makes mistakes because he thinks about too many things at once. He is interfered with by his own thoughts and feelings.

NAR (Narrow Effective Focus)

High scorers indicate that they are able to narrow attention effectively when the situation calls for it.

RED (Errors of Underinclusion)

High scores have chronically narrowed attention. They make mistakes because they cannot broaden attention when they need to.

---

those of another person. The height of your scale score would have some relevance only if it were compared with the scores of a large group of individuals participating in the same sport. Of much more importance than the elevation of a particular scale is the *profile configuration,* the elevation of one scale relative to the scores you make on other scales. It's critical how you describe your own strengths and weaknesses—in other words, how you compare your ability to make effective use of a broad attention focus with your tendency to make errors because your focus is too broad. Thus, look at the position of the Broad-External scale (BET) in comparison to the External Overload (OET); the Broad-Internal (BIT) in comparison to the Internal Overload

(OIT); the Narrow Effective Focus (NAR) relative to the tendency to make Errors of Underinclusion (RED). The average person scores equally high on both scales once they are plotted on the profile. Good attenders score higher on the scales indicating effective functioning (BET, BIT, NAR) than they do on scales indicating ineffective functioning (OET, OIT, RED).

The complete version of the test you just took is called the Test of Attentional and Interpersonal Style (TAIS).[1] It is much longer, containing 144 items, and thus the results or scores on the complete test are far more reliable indicators of attention than scores on this brief test. By administering the complete TAIS to a large number of athletes and then analyzing their answers, it was possible to identify several major attentional styles. Some of these styles are presented, beginning with the one in Figure 5.2.

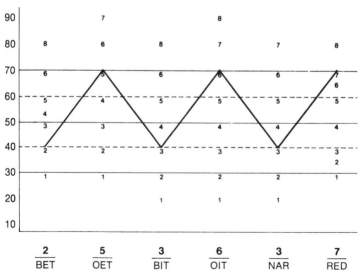

Figure 5.2   Ineffective Attentional Profile

The athlete whose profile appears in Figure 5.2 differs from an optimal performer in two very important ways. First, high scores on the OET and OIT scales indicate that he cannot deal with a large number of stimuli without becoming overloaded and confused. His low score on the NAR indicates that he cannot narrow attention in order to avoid becoming overloaded. Secondly, he is unable to shift attention from an internal focus to an external one when the situation requires it. For example, let's look at some of the difficulties a hitter with this profile has. First, he has great difficulty narrowing attention and focusing on the ball. Instead, when focused externally, he is aware of everything from the crowd noises to the movement of players on the field. Such a broad focus makes it difficult to concentrate on hitting the ball. Another problem occurs because he doesn't balance his internal and external attention. Instead he becomes trapped in his thoughts and responds to what is going on around him without thinking. In this case he may be so busy trying to analyze the situation, in an attempt to predict the next pitch, that he doesn't realize that the pitcher is already in his windup. The result is that he isn't ready when the ball arrives. He fails to shift to an external focus when he needs that kind of focus.

Athletes with this profile can learn to improve their performance by learning to narrow their attention and by learning to shift the direction of their focus. One procedure which would be helpful in accomplishing these goals is meditation (see Chapter 8). In addition to meditation, athletes with this attentional style would benefit from learning how to mentally rehearse their performance (see Chapter 9). Mental rehearsal procedures combined with meditation can be used to teach these athletes to distinguish between the relevant cues (the baseball) and the irrelevant ones (crowd noises).

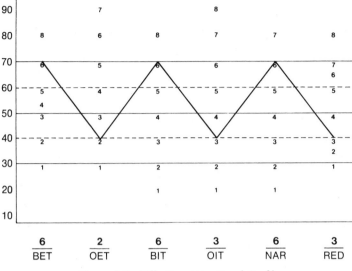

Figure 5.3   Effective Attentional Profile

Athletes with profile configurations like the one in Figure 5.3, provided they have responded honestly to the test, are optimal performers as far as attentional processes are concerned. Of course profiles like this one *can be faked* if the person is trying to look good or if he has an unrealistically high opinion of himself, but since the person taking the test usually wants help, cheating is rarely a problem. If the profile is an *accurate* one, it usually belongs to a superior athlete.

The profile presented in Figure 5.4 is that of a theoretical average athlete. The flat line indicates that he is average with respect to his ability to narrow or broaden attention and with respect to his tendency to make errors. There is no single outstanding strength or weakness here. Since no particular type of problem predominates, any adjustments

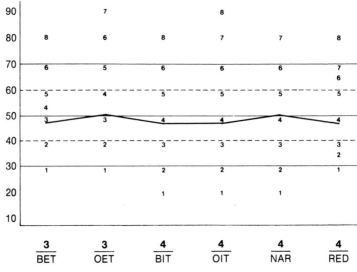

Figure 5.4 "Average" Profile

the athlete might want to make in his performance, theoretically speaking, would be based on his coach's preference for a particular method or because of a desire to develop a particular skill due to its relevance to a sport. For example, a quarterback might wish to improve his ability to broaden attention because he hasn't been spotting all the open receivers.

In point of fact, however, profiles like that presented in Figure 5.4 do not occur very often. Most of us have a particular style and tend to make specific types of errors. An important point to keep in mind, therefore, is that this average profile in no way imples that the individual shouldn't be working to improve his attentional processes. Unlike those super individuals who describe themselves as effective and as not making attentional errors, the average individual does make mistakes.

Figure 5.5 is associated with athletes who have a narrowed attentional focus and who have a tendency to "choke." They make mistakes in complex, rapidly changing situations because they fail to react quickly enough. In basketball they have difficulty finding the open man, or deciding if they should drive or take a jump shot. In football they don't adjust to shifts by the opposing team. Individuals with this profile would have difficulty trying to function as a wishbone quarterback—*especially* in the complex wishbone formations of today—or as the playmaker on a basketball or hockey team.

Happily there are two procedures which can help these

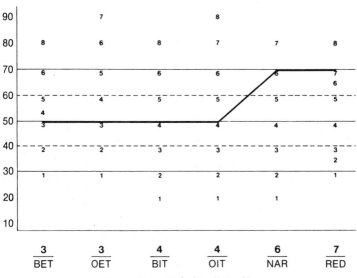

Figure 5.5 "Choking" Profile

athletes broaden their attention. First the individuals must be taught to relax. Arousal narrows an individual's attentional focus, but relaxation broadens it, and biofeedback training, progressive relaxation, hypnosis—all of which are described in detail in subsequent chapters—can be used for this purpose. In addition, mental rehearsal procedures are helpful because they can be used to teach an athlete to make more effective use of his narrowed focus. By learning to rapidly shift and direct a narrowed attentional focus to many different cues, a broad focus can be simulated. The trick, as we will see later on, is to be able to select the important cues to focus on and to ignore the others.

If you have a profile like the one presented in Figure 5.6, your major attentional strength is that you are able to analyze competitive situations and can plan out moves in advance. This strength, however, is also a weakness because you tend to make mistakes by becoming caught up in your own thoughts and lose awareness of what is going on around you. Your broad internal focus keeps you so involved in analyzing that you fail to respond to your environment. In effect you overanalyze and are still planning what to do when it's time to do it.

The best remedy here is to teach the athlete to be more aware of—and responsive to—external cues. As an example, baseball is a game in which there are many opportunities for players to drift away mentally from the game because they spend so much time standing around waiting for something to happen. Partially in response to this, players have developed ways to help keep their thoughts on the ball game. First of all they are constantly talking to the pitcher and to the batter, depending on which side is batting. Their chatter is designed to keep them and the other ball players alert. The custom of running out to your

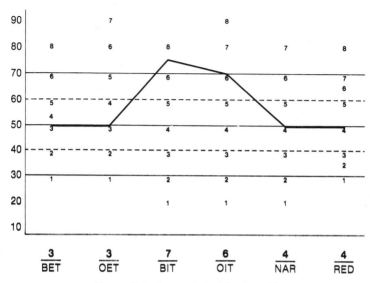

Figure 5.6 Internal Overload Profile

position on the field and then back to the dugout also helps because it keeps the player physically active, increases arousal slightly (unless the game is terribly one-sided), and helps concentration. Players also develop their own behavior patterns designed to get them to keep their thoughts from drifting away. Some players continually pound at their glove with their fist, others kick the ground, still others chew gum or tobacco. All of these, if used properly, can serve to break that internal focus and get the player's mind back on the game.

If you have a profile like that in Figure 5.7, you tend to be reactive rather than reflective—that is, you respond almost instinctively to changes in your environment. However, if your response is incorrect, you may fail to learn

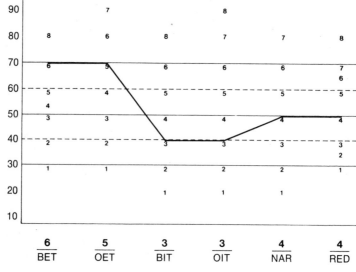

Figure 5.7   External Distractibility Profile

from it. When the same situation presents itself again, you then respond without reflection—as though you have never been in the situation before. Biofeedback procedures and rehearsal techniques can be used to train you to develop more of an internal (reflective) focus. Finally, athletes with profiles like the one in Figure 5.7 are more susceptible to being psyched out than those with a reflective style like the one in Figure 5.6 because they act on impulse to each new situation.

The final profile to be discussed is the one presented in Figure 5.8. If this is your profile, then you have a tendency to be your own worst enemy. You're likely to become upset by your mistakes and to think about little else, forgetting about the things which are going on around you. This overly internalized focus results in what is commonly called

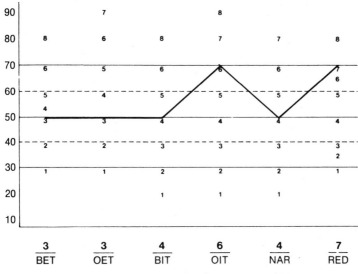

Figure 5.8   Choking–High Anxiety Profile

"choking." In psychological terms, by narrowing attention to your errors and by continuing to focus internally while the game is still going on, you're a sure bet to commit an ever increasing number of errors in the game. For this individual, timeouts may offer some relief, but the real blessing is when the game ends.

At the University of Rochester we examined the attentional styles of a considerable number of athletes. We then went to their various coaches and asked them (without their having any knowledge whatsoever of the test results) to rate the athletes' ability to perform under a variety of conditions. Dramatically enough, what we found was that those athletes with an attentional profile like the one presented in Figure 5.8 were described by the coaches as follows: "'choking,' inconsistent, falling apart under pressure, and unable to overcome early mistakes." To take up an earlier point, the athletes just described probably suffer from high levels of both state and trait anxiety. In other words, they are anxious human beings, and it has been our experience that through reducing the athletes' level of arousal, we can modify their attentional processes.

More specifically, many times athletes who "choke" would benefit from some external stimulus that would countermand their negative internal focus. Because these individuals are highly anxious, their attention is locked in on inappropriate things, and procedures such as hypnosis and biofeedback—which make few demands on them for implementation and which continually direct their attention externally—are most helpful.

Once the negative (anxiety equals "choking") set is broken, the athlete can regain some control over his attentional process and can then *begin* to assume more responsibility for directing the course of his training. It may take some time for this training to produce results. Accordingly, if you find you have this type of profile, learn how to practice some relaxation and reflective or meditative procedures in order to prevent additional problems from developing. The importance of this is not to be underestimated. You *can* maintain attentional control so long as you control arousal. It isn't simple, of course, since to do this you must learn to recognize and offset anxiety before it gets out of hand.

There are obviously many other possible attentional profiles. The few profiles that I've described do occur fairly often and provide a good illustration of the way in which an individual's attentional style can be used to predict potential problem areas and to suggest methods for dealing with them. Hopefully by now you should have begun to develop some deep interest about your own anxiety level and how it affects your attentional processes. In the next few chapters the various procedures mentioned here—biofeedback, hypnosis, and mental rehearsal—are presented in much detail. The hope is that with the information you have gained about your own responses to stress and your attentional style, you are now in a position to select one or two of these procedures and use them to improve your performance. Other athletes have done so—so why not you?

Chapter Six. **Hypnosis**

I can't think of a single psychological procedure that has been used as widely as hypnosis[1] and yet has remained so misunderstood by professionals and laymen alike. The mention of the word is enough to conjure up visions of mystical and even supernatural influence. For instance, a few years ago I was invited to appear on a TV talk show, and after a brief discussion about the importance of mental preparation, which included mention of hypnosis, I was accused by the hostess of the show of interfering with man's "God-given abilities." She felt that it was unfair that some athletes should have the benefit of psychological preparation while others did not. Moreover she stated unequivocally that for athletes to be psychologically prepared was "unnatural."

As we continued to talk, I learned a great deal about my hostess. This TV appearance was occurring just after the first Muhammad Ali–Ken Norton fight, which Norton won. After his victory it had been announced that as part of his preparation for the fight, Norton had been to see a hypnotist. As it turned out, my interviewer admired Ali a great deal and believed that Norton had been able to get an unfair advantage through his use of the hypnotist. She really believed hypnosis allowed Norton to transcend his own natural ability. This belief was reinforced both by her own lack of knowledge about hypnosis and by her feelings that Ali was no ordinary mortal. She apparently could not accept the idea that her hero could be beaten by a normal human being. This sentiment, combined with the mystique surrounding hypnosis, had convinced her that Norton's psychological preparation was unnatural. I spent the next fifteen minutes trying to convince her this was not the case—in vain.

Like the hostess on the talk show, I once held the belief that hypnosis was some supernatural phenomenon. I believed that the hypnotist had some special magical power which he could use for good or evil. My beliefs were certainly reinforced by the sensationalism associated with hypnosis in the press, but they were based mostly on what I had seen in demonstrations of hypnosis.

As a youth I had seen hypnotists cause people to do many strange things: become paralyzed; hallucinate people or objects which weren't there; get drunk on water; eat onions, thinking they were apples; and other bizarre behavior. I also knew that at one time hypnosis had been used as the only anesthesia in many major surgical operations, including the amputation of arms and legs. And nothing in my own experience prepared me to believe that such things were possible under normal conditions.

Since that time I have learned that hypnosis may provide a circumstance within which people do and experience things that they don't usually experience at other times. Hypnosis *allows* them to do things; it does not *give* them power or *cause* them to excel. I have also learned that other techniques (meditation, biofeedback, autogenic training) can be used to allow people to do similar things.

I pointed out earlier that to break a board you need a minimal amount of strength and some knowledge of technique. More important than that, however, you need to have faith to trust in what you are being told and have the courage to attempt the feat. The faith, trust, and courage are all mental and they are directly related to your ability to control your attention. Until you try breaking the board, however, the act retains a certain amount of mysticism for you. In a similar way, until you experience hypnosis, it will remain a mystery.

What Is Hypnosis?

Hypnosis, although it is indeed a very useful and impressive tool, is nothing more than a cooperative venture between the hypnotist and the subject. The athlete, by going along with the verbal suggestions of the hypnotist, discovers and experiences things about himself that he had not been aware of previously. This new awareness occurs because the conditions around him optimize his ability to concentrate and direct attentional processes.

Actually most of us have experienced feelings similar to the ones individuals experience when they are hypnotized. Occasionally, in reading a book or watching a movie, you may become so caught up in the story that all awareness of where you are sitting and what is going on around you is gone because of your total focus on the story or movie. Then too, just before you go off to sleep, you may experience a state not unlike hypnosis. You are completely relaxed in bed, drifting along with your thoughts, and suddenly the telephone rings. In this hypnoticlike state you aren't sure whether the phone is actually ringing or you are dreaming. It often takes a second or third ring for you to realize the phone really is ringing.

Not infrequently, people who have been hypnotized are questioned about it afterward and they express disbelief about having been in a hypnotic state. What happens is that the hypnotist performs an induction—that is, he presents a series of suggestions designed to get the subject to relax and enter a passive, receptive frame of mind. Once this passive, reflective state is achieved, the hypnotist makes some specific suggestions. For example, he suggests that an imaginary fly or mosquito is bothering the person or that he will be unable to bend his arm or that he will forget his name. While hypnotized, the subject responds to these suggestions—he swats at the fly, fails to bend his arm when challenged to do so, or forgets his name. Yet in spite of witnesses to these events, people still refuse to believe that they have been hypnotized, and the primary reason for this is because they expect the experience during hypnosis to be something other than what it is. Again, the mystique prevails.

For instance, individuals being hypnotized for the first time expect to be put in a trance. They mistakenly believe that they should feel as if they are floating in space; they expect to hear a powerful voice coming out of the darkness ordering them to do things or granting them some power. In contrast to their expectations, however, they find that hypnosis is not a trance state. Yet some very remarkable things are made to occur through the use of hypnotic suggestions. In addition to what has been already mentioned, hypnotic suggestions have also been used to cure skin rashes, to lower the amount of insulin diabetics need, and to help people remember or forget. Quite obviously hypnosis can be a powerful tool.

In talking about hypnosis and its use in athletics, it's helpful to explain the procedure in terms of four phases. The first phase involves the induction of the hypnotic state—in other words, the instructions given to the subject to prepare him for phase two. Phase two is the hypnotic state—the period of time during which hypnotic work or suggestions are given. This is followed by phase three, which involves nothing more than waking the subject up. The final phase is the posthypnotic phase. Very often the suggestions given in phase two are expected to affect the subject in phase four.

Hypnotic Induction

Induction procedures are fairly standard. They are comprised of a series of suggestions aimed at eliciting the subject's cooperation and at directing his attention to thoughts and feelings which are often associated with being relaxed and peaceful. Hypnotists employ a wide variety of equipment and techniques in order to facilitate the induction process. The selection of a particular induction procedure is made either because the hypnotist feels personally comfortable with it or because he feels the subject's attentional style or personality will be more susceptible to it. For example, some hypnotists have subjects fix their eyes on an object. This may be a spot on the wall, a spinning wheel, a coin, or a religious or mystical symbol. Here the hypnotist uses the subject's religious or magical beliefs as well as the strain on his eyes to develop the subject's confidence in the procedure. As the subject begins to strain his eyes in order to look at the object, the hypnotist offers suggestions that his eyes are becoming tired. Soon suggestions are made to get the subject to close his eyes, and then standard hypnotic suggestions are given. Some hypnotists, employing a more scientific approach, use a strobe light. The light is set to flash at a frequency somewhere between eight and thirteen times a second. Often the subject is told that the light is flashing at the same frequency as alpha rhythms, which are the brain waves associated with being awake but relaxed. The subject is told that through a process called photic driving, it is possible to use the light to cause him to develop alpha rhythms and thus enter a hypnotic trance. As with the eye-closure technique above, subjects eventually tire of looking at the light. They close their eyes, and then standard suggestions for deepening the hypnotic state are given.

The following procedure is one that I have used with a fair amount of success. The subject is asked to sit in a comfortable chair and to relax as much as possible. After being instructed to close his eyes he is asked to extend his right arm at shoulder height. Then he is told to turn his hand over so that his palm is up. Next he is asked to imagine that he is holding a ball in his hand and is told that as he becomes more and more relaxed the arm holding the ball will become heavier and heavier. Finally the subject is instructed that once the arm, in response to the suggestions of heaviness, touches the chair he will be deeply asleep.

I like this particular procedure because it is subject-paced—that is, the subject decides how fast he is becoming hypnotized. This serves two very important purposes. First it allows the subject to feel as though he has an active role in the process. This can be crucial when working with athletes, because they are competitive and may need to feel as though they have some control over what is transpiring. In addition it allows the hypnotist to follow the condition of the subject and to pace his induction and suggestions accordingly.

If you have not experienced hypnosis and are curious about it, you *can* try it yourself. Using a tape recorder, record the following induction and awaking procedure in slow, measured tones. Obviously the induction, since it is being read onto a tape, cannot be paced accurately for each person. You may find that you have your hands down while the tape is still giving instructions to lower your arm. The inverse may also occur—you may find that you have not lowered your arm completely when this segment of the tape ends. Should either of these occur, don't worry, simply relax and let yourself concentrate on those suggestions that are appropriate for you. If your hand is already down, just relax and let yourself float along until the next part of the tape is reached.

I would like to introduce a word of caution here. If you have any trepidation about listening to these instructions without having a trained hypnotist present, then don't do so—for a variety of reasons.

To take an extreme example, I had a student come up to me (this occurred only once in about 1,000 inductions, so it's not at all common) just prior to an induction, telling me she was afraid she might have a seizure (she was epileptic) if hypnotized. I told her that this typically did not occur, but if she became at all concerned during the induction, she could just open her eyes and ignore the rest of the procedure (it was a group induction of about fifty students). She did continue to worry about the possibility of a seizure and began to feel dizzy, so she opened her eyes and waited while the rest of the class continued. Her worry and concern unfortunately kept her from responding in the usual way, but wherever any serious concerns exist, there should be no attempt to get involved in the procedure without an expert present.

However, as you can see by reading through the induction procedure, there is nothing mystical, surprising, or frightening about what is going to take place. By listening to and cooperating with the tape that you yourself make, you will be able to relax and demonstrate to yourself what it feels like to be hypnotized.

Induction Procedure

All right now I want you to sit down in a comfortable chair.... Your arms and legs should be resting comfortably. Your arms are relaxed either in your lap or on the arms of the chair.... Your feet should be flat on the floor or else comfortably supported.

You are about to find that by listening to these words and by letting your thoughts go in the directions that are suggested that you will be able to experience what it is like to be hypnotized....

Once you are comfortable, just close your eyes and relax all of the muscles in your body.... That's fine, just close your eyes.... Now begin breathing deeply ... and slowly.... Inhale deeply ... and exhale slowly.... As you exhale you will begin to feel your entire body relax.... Notice as you exhale how much more relaxed your arms ... legs ... neck ... shoulders ... and face become.

That's fine.... Now take your right arm and extend it out in front of you at shoulder height.... Turn your right hand so that the palm of your hand is facing up.... That's fine.... Now I want you to imagine that you are holding a heavy ball in your right hand.... Curl your fingers up and feel the ball.... As you continue to hold the ball, you will find that it becomes heavier and heavier. Finally, when you can no longer hold up the ball, your hand will touch the

chair or your lap. At that moment you will completely relax, the ball will be gone, and you will be deeply asleep. . . .

Now listen carefully to the things I say to you. . . . Listen
carefully to the things that I say. . . . As you continue to
hold the ball, relax the rest of your body. . . . Relax the
muscles in your left arm, relax the muscles in your left
hand, and fingers. . . . Relax the muscles in your legs, in
your calves, and in your thighs. . . . Continue breathing
deeply and slowly, and as you exhale notice how much
heavier the ball becomes. . . . Just relax and let yourself
go. . . . If your mind wanders that's all right, just bring it
back to the things that I say. . . .

While I have been talking, you have probably noticed
that your arm has become heavier and heavier. . . . Your
right arm is very heavy and tired. . . . The more you try and
hold it up, the heavier it becomes. . . . It would be so pleasant just to let yourself go, to completely relax. . . . Once
your arm touches the chair, you will be able to completely
relax. . . . Your arm is very heavy and tired. . . . It is tired
from holding up that heavy ball. . . . You are trying to hold
it up, but the harder you try, the more difficult it becomes. . . . The harder you try, the more difficult it becomes. . . . Your arm is drifting down, down, down. Once
the arm reaches the chair you will completely relax and fall
deep asleep. . . .

It is hard work trying to hold up a ball as heavy as the
one in your hand. . . . You lift it up just a bit, but then your
hand lowers more. . . . It's a losing battle. . . . It's as if you
are walking up an endless hill of sand. . . . Each time you
push the ball up, it pushes you back down. . . . The ball is so
heavy . . . so heavy. . . . It will be so nice when your arm
touches and you completely relax. . . . (Ten-second pause.)

You have worked very hard and you have done a good
job, but now you deserve a rest. Don't resist any longer. . . .

If your hand has not already touched, it soon would have. . . . You have worked very hard, but now it is time to let your hand down. Put your hand down, the ball is no longer there. . . . Put your hand down and let yourself go . . . deep asleep . . . deep asleep. . . .

Listen carefully to the things I say. . . . I am going to help you become even more relaxed . . . more deeply asleep. . . . Now that you can rest your arm, it will be easy to become much more deeply asleep. . . . Just relax and remember that no matter how deeply asleep you become, you will always be able to hear the sound of my voice. . . . I am going to count from one to five, and with each count, you will find yourself becoming more deeply asleep. . . . With each count, you will fall deeper and deeper asleep.

One . . . breathing deeply and slowly . . . completely relaxed . . . deeply asleep. . . . Two . . . deeper and deeper asleep . . . deeper . . . still deeper asleep. . . . Three . . . down . . . down . . . down . . . deeper and deeper asleep. . . . Four . . . completely relaxed and deep asleep. . . . Five . . . deep asleep. . . .

Even though you are deeply asleep, you can still hear my voice . . . you can move . . . and you can even talk without waking up. . . . Even though you are deep asleep, you will find that you can move and still remain just as deeply asleep as you are right now. . . . Now I am going to give you a chance to experience how closely your thoughts and movements are related. . . . I am going to give you a chance to experience how closely your thoughts and movements are related. . . . If you listen carefully and follow these instructions, you will find that you are able to have the experience that I will describe to you. . . .

Extend both arms out in front of you at shoulder height. . . . Extend both arms out in front of you at shoulder height. . . . Your palms are facing each other, and your hands are about six inches apart.... That's fine.... Now imagine that your hands are two giant magnets pushing against each other.... Notice how strong the feelings are as your hands push away from each other.... The feelings are becoming stronger ... and stronger... and stronger.... Your hands are being pushed farther, and farther, and farther apart.... You may try and keep them close together, but the harder you try, the stronger they push against each other.... Harder and harder... farther and farther apart.... (Ten-second pause.)

That's fine.... Now relax... relax.... Your hands are no longer magnets.... Bring them back together and notice how far they have moved.... Your thoughts alone caused your hands to move apart.... Now return your hands to the chair or your lap and completely relax.... Your hands are no longer magnets, return them to the chair and completely relax....

In a moment I am going to wake you up.... When I do, you will find that you feel very comfortable and relaxed.... You will remember everything that has happened and you will have enjoyed the experience.... I am going to wake you up, and when I do, you will feel comfortable and relaxed, and you will be looking forward to the rest of the day.... I will wake you up by counting from ten to one.... By the time I get to five you will be waking up.... When I get to three, you will begin stretching your arms and legs.... On the count of two you will open your eyes.... On the count of one you will be wide awake.... You will feel very comfortable, you will be wide awake, and you will have enjoyed this experience.... Ten.... Nine.... Eight .... You are slowly beginning to wake up.... Seven.... Becoming more awake. ... Six.... Five.... You are waking up.... Four.... More and more awake. ... Three.... Stretch your legs and arms.... Two.... Open your eyes ...

open your eyes. . . . One! . . . Wide awake! . . . Eyes open,
you feel very comfortable and ready for the rest of the day.

The induction procedure that has just been presented is
only a small portion of what is actually involved in the use
of hypnosis to improve athletics. What occurs between the
end of the induction and the waking of the subject is critical
because once you have been hypnotized, then specific
suggestions can be given to assist you in improving your
performance. Please bear in mind that any suggestions described during the course of this chapter were intended for
particular athletes in particular situations, and they do not
apply to anyone else.

Posthypnotic Suggestion

Many of the suggestions of the hypnotist are designed to be
effective after the subject has been awakened. Such suggestions are called posthypnotic and have been used extensively in sports. Posthypnotic suggestions usually focus on
the way the athlete should feel in a certain competitive
situation. For example, needing to improve his control,
one of the New York Mets' pitchers underwent hypnosis
and was told that he would find himself putting a little more
pressure on the ball with one of his fingers. In a similar way
a hitter in baseball might be instructed, "The next time you
step into the batter's box, you will feel comfortable and
relaxed. Your neck and shoulders will be loose and your
swing will be smooth. You will find it easy to concentrate
on the ball and you will be amazed at how clearly you see
the ball." In swimming, a diver might be told, "During the
meet you will find yourself feeling relaxed and comfortable.
Your thoughts will be on how good you feel and on how

great it feels to get maximum lift out of the board and to have complete control over your body in the air. Thoughts of the situation, the meet, or the crowd will not interfere with the joys of diving." It is paramount in giving posthypnotic suggestions that they not be generalized, but rather they should be limited to particular times or situations. For example, the instructions given to the diver were strictly predicated on the understanding that the diver knew the dives he was to execute in the meet so well that he did not have to think about them. If this were not the case, then attention during the competition would have to focus more on the mechanics of the dive. For that matter, if the hypnotist's instructions were carried over into a practice session involving new dives, they actually could interfere with the diver's ability to concentrate on developing a new technique or dive.

A second, seemingly very important factor in the use of posthypnotic suggestions is the length of time that they are intended to remain in effect, but unfortunately there is no way of predicting this since their effectiveness varies from person to person and is affected by the specific nature of the suggestions themselves. In any case, it would be dangerous to employ specific hypnotic suggestions in a game. Since time intervals may range dramatically from a few minutes to several months, it's probably fair to say that the more relevant the suggestion to performance, and the more frequently it is used, the longer it is likely to remain. As an example, a suggestion about being relaxed in the batter's box, if it is effective, results in an increase in the confidence of the athlete. This increase in confidence acts to further lower tension levels, which in turn may help the suggestion to have a long-lasting effect.

As noted earlier, suggestions given during hypnosis can be focused on creating the appropriate feelings, thoughts, or attitudes either during the hypnotic state or after the subject wakes up. In most instances both procedures are employed. For example, hypnosis can be used to improve an individual's memory during the hypnotic state and thus to relive past experiences while still hypnotized. This recalled experience is retained after the subject wakes up, and coupled with posthypnotic suggestions, can help bring about behavior changes.

The heightened recall which subjects are capable of during hypnosis can be very important when working with an athlete who has fears in a particular competitive situation. The hypnotist assists the athlete in remembering the experience that initially created his fear. For example, it may be that he was injured one time when he was jumping to catch a pass in the middle of several defenders, and now, instead of focusing all his attention on the ball, he finds himself listening for the footsteps of defenders. Therefore, when the athlete is in the hypnotic state, the hypnotist gives suggestions designed to reeducate him. He points out that the subject has caught hundreds of passes before without injury. He then suggests that the best way to avoid injury is to be able to relax. Relaxation is impossible, the athlete is then told, so long as he is afraid of being hit and so long as he is anxiously listening for the footsteps of his opponents. Gradually the athlete's confidence is restored. Then posthypnotic suggestions are given to assist the athlete in maintaining that confidence out on the field. For example, he is told, "You will find that as you jump to receive the ball, your entire body feels comfortable and relaxed. You will be able to see the ball clearly, and you will watch it so closely that you will see the laces spinning as it comes toward you. You will watch as it touches your hands, and you will feel the ball as you pull it in and hold it tightly against yourself."

Remember the weight lifter who, as he was lifting 405 pounds during a national competition, thought that it felt like 260 pounds, the weight he lifted so easily in practice. You'll recall that these thoughts caused him to relax his grip and that he dropped the weight. Following this experience, he found his confidence and concentration disturbed. He came to me for treatment. Hypnosis in effect enabled him to relive the experience, but with a different outcome. He was told to alter his response so that he reacted to the lightness of the bar by bearing down and lifting harder. In addition posthypnotic suggestions were given to offset his fear of not keeping his grip on the bar—he was told that when he grabbed the bar, he would feel so secure and his hands would grip the bar so firmly that he would feel as though they were part of the bar. And when it was time for him to release the bar, his hands would relax and return to normal.

Unfortunately this did not provide all the answers for this individual. He did well for a while, but then—a disaster. In a particularly big meet he was getting ready to go up for his final lift with a winning total. All the other athletes knew about this individual's fear of slipping and dropping the bar, and, as he stood there concentrating just prior to the lift, the manager of one of the other competitors ran up and moved him away from the bar. The manager then bent over and pretended to brush some dust from the bar. The athlete failed to make the lift, but not because his hands slipped. His concentration was so disturbed that he couldn't find the strength and coordination to get under the bar—a classic psych job!

In addition to increasing the athlete's self-confidence and decreasing his fear, there are other ways hypnotic suggestions can be used to improve performance. Two areas in particular appear very promising. In a crisis situation the hypnotist may intervene and redirect the athlete's attention. In another situation, the hypnotist may work with the athlete to increase his tolerance for pain. Let's consider the crisis situation first.

Hypnosis and Crisis Intervention

When an individual is upset, he loses the ability to direct and control the attentional processes which reduce anxiety and enable him to perform effectively. What is needed is a powerful external stimulus which controls the athlete's attention long enough for a calming process to begin. We've all seen scenes where a hysterical person receives a sharp slap in the face or a thorough shaking from someone trying to stop his hysterical state. A hypnotist who has the confidence of an athlete can function in the same way (and less painfully) by demanding and directing the attention of the person who is upset. This doesn't mean that coaches and parents, if they have the confidence of the athlete and they themselves don't become upset, can't perform this same initial refocusing of attention, but the hypnotist, because of his experience, may be able to do this more quickly. More important still, once attention is refocused, the hypnotist turns the crisis situation into a constructive growth experience for the athlete through suggestions.

An example of crisis intervention can be seen in the 1974 World Ice Skating Championships in Germany. One of the U.S. competitors became upset because the crowd began booing just as she was about to make her appearance. Actually they were booing the judges for the low marks that had been awarded to the previous skater, but this competitor thought the booing was being directed at her, and she began sobbing uncontrollably. She was eventually calmed down by her coach and was able to go on to win a silver medal. Although no hypnotist was involved, her situation provides a good framework for examining what happens to you in a crisis situation and how hypnotic suggestions can be used to overcome the crisis.

What happens to you in a crisis situation? Generally, some stimulus (in this case the crowd's boos) causes you to become anxious and overwhelmed by your own thoughts and feelings. Your attention gets out of control and begins to turn inward, and your inability to control your own thoughts becomes very frightening. You may feel dizzy because you are trying to keep up with everything going on inside your head. You find yourself thinking irrationally, jumping from thought to thought in a crazy, fragmented way, and if we were to get inside your head, the inner dialogue might sound like this: "What's happening? I'm dizzy—why are they booing? I'm supposed to be skating! I can't think—what's the matter with me? I have to skate— what's my routine? How could they do this to me?" At this stage, unfortunately, the more you try to pull your thoughts together, the more overloaded and out of control you become.

As the crisis point is reached, you will become unusually receptive to suggestions. In effect the crisis situation acts in many ways like a hypnotic induction procedure. The major difference is that in hypnosis you voluntarily give up control to the hypnotist, whereas in a crisis your anxiety involuntarily throws you out of control. Because of this loss of control and your fear over what is happening, you are susceptible to any suggestions or advice that promise to reinstate order and explain what has happened to you. The crisis has led to the development of a hypnoticlike state even though no formal induction was instituted.

The individual who is out of control will often respond to any person who breaks through his confusion in the same way he would respond to a hypnotist. However, because of the hypersuggestibility that develops during a crisis, the experience can be either a very positive or a very negative one for an athlete. If the individual breaking through is also upset or if he happens to offer destructive suggestions ("You'll never be able to perform, now you've blown it"), permanent damage can be done to the athlete's self-confidence and ability to perform. On the other hand a calm, thoughtful person—whether parent, coach, team-mate, or professional—can turn the crisis into a positive growth-oriented experience.

Although crisis situations are rather uncommon exam-ples of the hypnoticlike state, they do occur, and because they have such a profound effect on the individual, it be-comes worthwhile to deal with them in more detail. There are several rules that should be followed when attempting to deal with a crisis situation. Let me outline them and then I'll show them in action.

First, the hypnotist, parent, or coach, regardless of what he may actually be feeling, must be able to maintain an outward appearance of calm. Second, he must know how to break through the athlete's confused state of mind—how to get his attention. Third, to avoid further confusion, he must keep his communications short and simple. This means he must stick to one or two reassuring thoughts and avoid becoming distracted by the athlete's confusion. He should *not* try to deal with specific doubts or fears at this point. Fourth, he must be able to redirect the athlete's negative internal attentional focus toward positive expectancies. Quite obviously the crisis has raised the athlete's arousal level and in so doing has narrowed his attentional focus. His ability to shift voluntarily from internal to external stimuli has been impaired and his attention has become locked onto internally generated negative thoughts and feelings. Interestingly enough, it's possible for the person intervening to use the same arousal the crisis generated to get the athlete to lock onto those external stimuli and attitudes which are important for his performance. Finally, following the performance itself, the individual who has been working with the athlete should take the time to turn what has happened into a positive experience by pointing out how the athlete was able to cope with it, what he learned from it, and how he will be a better person because of it. Now, to see this process in action let's take a situation like the World Ice Skating Championships and examine one way of dealing with it.

As the coach, you look up to see that your skater is upset, crying, skating in aimless little circles, talking to herself, and clenching and unclenching her fists. You don't become upset because you know that you are capable of breaking through to the skater and of eventually turning this crisis into a positive experience. You step in front of the skater, take her by the shoulders, and in a firm voice call her name, "Jane! Jane!" At this point, remarkably enough, you have already done several things that will allow you to break through and grab the skater's attention. First, by stepping in front of her, you have blocked off many visual stimuli which may be adding to her confusion. In addition, by stopping her from skating around you have decreased both the physical sensations and the emotional intensity she is experiencing. In effect all her visual attention is now directed toward you. By putting your hands on her shoulders, you are creating a powerful stimulus that draws her attention toward you—and away from her own confusing thoughts and feelings. Finally, by calling her name, you are auditorily gaining her attention. Her name is a very strong stimulus for her because she has been responding to it her entire life.

At this point there's a momentary lull and she's quiet. However, as she begins to recognize you, there's a rush to confide all her fears and feelings. If you try to deal with any of this, you only increase the amount of information she has to cope with by adding the proverbial fuel to the proverbial fire. Instead you gently say, "Later, later," and quietly insist that she engage in some activity that helps her calm down. Thus you find yourself speaking like this, "Listen to me! Listen to me! I want you to breathe deeply and slowly.... Breathe deeply and slowly.... That's fine! That's fine! Don't worry—it'll be all right! It will be all right! Breathe deeply and slowly . . . deeply and slowly—good!"

As the young woman begins to respond to the suggestion to breathe deeply and slowly, she becomes calmer. Once again, there's an attempt on her part to describe what has happened. Although she is now in a better position to handle that discussion, it's still not the time to do so. That should be communicated in a comforting manner and she should feel assured that you will hear all she has to say later on. The fact that she now has enough control of herself to follow your instructions to breathe deeply and slowly should prompt you to begin refocusing her attention on positive things. The communication can become a little more complex—but don't get too ambitious. It's still best to stick to one or two suggestions.

"That's fine.... Now you're in control.... I knew you would be. Now let's show them how you can skate.... They made you mad, but you'll show them! They'll be standing and applauding when you're finished! Show them what kind of a skater you really are!" These suggestions present the skater with a brief interpretation of some of her feelings and hopefully transform her fear into anger. Now the narrowed attentional focus previously directed towards fears of failure and loss of control is redirected toward showing them "what kind of a skater you really are!" In effect she has gone from being psyched out to psyched up in just a couple of minutes.

Finally, after the performance is over and the skater comes off the ice, the coach congratulates her on the job she has done, even if she has failed. She is told—and this is absolutely true—that it took genuine strength and courage for her to go out on the ice after that initial upset. She magnificently demonstrated how much strength of character she really had. Because of this traumatic experience and because of her newfound strength, the next time something like this occurs, she will know that she *can* handle it. She need not be afraid in the future. Then, gradually, her almost disastrous response can be put in perspective. "You misinterpreted the boos of the crowd and took them personally. A natural enough response, and one that you have learned a great deal from. You don't learn and improve if you don't make mistakes. Because of this one, you'll be a better skater in the future."

Throughout this presentation of crisis situations, I have been describing procedures as though the coach or a parent were a competent hypnotist. In point of fact, under these crisis conditions they do function in a similar capacity and have the same potential control and influence over the subject. Obviously, because no formal induction procedure was used, no sleep suggestions were given, and because the athlete has not defined this as a hypnotic experience, it's not necessary to wake the person up.

Hypnosis and Injury

As mentioned earlier, hypnosis has also been used for the reduction of pain due to injuries during practice or competition. Only an accomplished hypnotist should get involved in these procedures. Briefly, following a standard induction procedure, the subject is given direct suggestions that focus on increasing the individual's tolerance to pain. A sample suggestion: "The pain in your leg is beginning to disappear. You may still feel a little pressure but the stiffness and soreness are going away. When you wake up, you will find that you are able to move the leg. You will feel good about being able to use your leg, and the pain and stiffness will be gone."

Some hypnotists prefer to induce anesthesia in part of the body first, usually in a hand, and will demonstrate the effectiveness of the procedure to the subject by sticking a sterilized pin in the back of the hand. The subject usually reports that the hand feels numb and tingly, as though it were shot with novocaine. Then the subject is told that he himself can transfer the anesthesia by touching various parts of his body with that hand. Following these instructions, the subject introduces his own anesthesia to the affected part of the body. This particular procedure has been helpful in dealing with a variety of painful injuries, including pulled muscles, bruises, and torn cartilages. The major advantage to this type of treatment, of course, is that it reduces dependence on medication, but the athlete has to be very careful that he doesn't begin playing his sport again before the injury has fully healed.

If this seems to border on the miraculous, let me say that there are a number of theories about how hypnosis acts to reduce pain. We do know that a great deal of the pain experienced by athletes is due to torn muscle tissue or to muscle spasms—which may not be detectable as such by the athlete.[1] One way that hypnosis probably works, therefore, is via the relaxation of those muscles that are aggravating the injured area or causing the experience of pain through contractions. In addition the suggestions given by the hypnotist often cause the subject to direct his attention in one of two ways. In one case he learns to describe the painful experience in an objective way, distancing himself from the feelings—and thus experiencing less pain. Or else he directs attention away from the painful area. When attention is focused on a painful stimulus and accompanied by fearful thoughts, muscle tension increases and the athlete becomes more and more sensitive to the pain. By reducing pain or redirecting attention or reinterpreting the experience (or by a combination of these), the hypnotist helps the athlete lower muscle tension and thus reduce pain. It doesn't sound simple, I know—and it sure isn't simple—but it does work. We've included hypnosis as part

Table 6.1   Uses of Hypnosis in Competitive Athletics

1. Treatment of fear through catharsis (ventilation of feelings associated with a past traumatic experience).
2. The use of heightened recall and visual imagery to increase self-confidence through reliving past successes.
3. Suggestions of relaxation to minimize anxiety during competition, when traveling, or in the presence of others.
4. Suggestions of anesthesia to reduce the pain associated with injuries.
5. Suggestions may be used to increase the subject's ability to concentrate and narrow attention in critical situations.
6. Suggestions of amnesia may be used to cause subjects to forget experiences that might interfere with performance.

of general relaxation procedures at the University of Rochester, using it to induce a state of relaxation and then to enhance visual imagery of carefully selected situations. When this is done effectively, it provides the following advantages to the athlete: control over arousal in competition, increased self-confidence, a greater willingness to take chances, and increased sensitivity to important feelings and environmental cues. Table 6.1 presents a summary of the ways hypnosis has been used successfully in athletics.

Problems Associated with Hypnosis

Although there really are many valuable applications of hypnosis to athletics, there are also some problems and dangers associated with its use. To begin with, research on the susceptibility of subjects to hypnotic suggestions indicates that ten per cent of the population does not respond at all, another ten per cent is capable of developing all the phenomena commonly associated with hypnosis, and the remaining eighty per cent fall somewhere in between these two extremes. Thus one terribly obvious major problem with the use of hypnosis is that any individual athlete in question may be incapable of responding to treatment. This is a reality and we have to recognize it.

A second reality has to do with the fact that a competent hypnotist needs to be available to the athlete, and there are, unfortunately, very few around. Ideally the use of hypnosis, like many other psychological procedures, should involve the athlete, the trainer, and/or the coach as well as the hypnotist. The presence of the trainer or coach is important because the hypnotist needs to know that the suggestions given will not interfere with the athlete's being able to respond to the specific demands of the competitive situation. Without a knowledge of these specific demands, the hypnotist might successfully respond to one of the athlete's immediate problems in ways that do *not* apply to competitive situations. Since this is an important point, let's have more than one example to illustrate how it works.

Pretend for the moment that you are a pro quarterback and you come to me because you are anxious. I hypnotize you and suggest that when you feel yourself becoming anxious, you can calm yourself down by breathing deeply and slowly and by relaxing all your muscles. Next weekend I turn on the TV set and watch in horror as you drop back for a pass, then suddenly stop and relax, letting your arms fall to your side while you begin breathing deeply and slowly. To relate it back to Chapter 3, the hypnotist must be sure that he does not give the athlete suggestions that could cause him to develop an attentional focus inappropriate for the competitive situation.

Another type of problem can occur if the hypnotist attempts to work without consulting the coach or trainer, and it falls in a much more serious realm. Although there are many occasions when using hypnosis as an anesthetic would seem appropriate, this is not always a good idea. Pain in most instances is experienced for a reason. It is a warning to the individual telling him to stop before he becomes permanently injured. For this reason the hypnotist must have the input as well as the consent of the team trainer and a physician prior to treating the athlete's pain. Many hypnotists in fact do not give suggestions that are designed to remove pain completely. Instead they suggest that the athlete retain enough feeling to know when he is injured.

Just as there can be problems when the hypnotist attempts to work without the benefit of information and advice from the coach or trainer, the reverse is also true. Although a coach or trainer is capable of inducing hypnosis with highly susceptible individuals or in crisis conditions, a certain amount of clinical training and experience is necessary in order to ensure the safety of the athlete. First of all the athlete's belief and confidence in the hypnotist is important, and it is more difficult to obtain positive consequences without this confidence. Thus the credentials of the hypnotist become important—and for reasons beyond this matter of confidence.

For instance, the surface problems which athletes seem to be having may not in fact be the real issues. With problems of anxiety it may appear as though the source of the anxiety is the competitive situation, whereas problems much more elemental than the competitive setting are the cause. When this happens, treatment is ineffectual and might even be negative in that its failure to help the athlete competitively could further undermine his self-confidence—e.g., "If he can't help me, I'm lost." In brief then, the clinical training of the hypnotist should help him identify the elements of a person's behavioral patterns which transcend the athletic situation.

Another strong argument for having an experienced hypnotist present is that the suggestions given to subjects, while they often seem obvious and straightforward, are always subject to the individual interpretation of the athlete. Suggestions are nothing more than words, yet the same words may mean vastly different things to two different individuals, and clearly it's important that both the hypnotist and the subject interpret the suggestions given in the same way. To take a fairly exaggerated, but not impossible example, I might suggest to a female athlete that her legs are becoming relaxed and heavy and feel nice and warm.

However, she may be sensitive about the size of her legs and interpret my suggestion as indicating that she is getting fat. This thought could upset her and would then interfere with her ability to follow other suggestions. The hypnotist's training and experience should allow him to recognize when suggestions are being misinterpreted and, equally important, when they are having a negative effect on the athlete.

The final major reason for using an experienced clinical hypnotist concerns the personality variables which come into play with the use of hypnosis. Although there is no truth to the belief that good hypnotic subjects are weak, dependent individuals, the hypnotic relationship—like any helping relationship—can foster or encourage dependency. At the same time that the athlete is going to the hypnotist and asking for help, the induction procedure and the suggestions made by the hypnotist require that for the time being the individual give control over to the hypnotist. During the session he allows himself to be a follower, responding to the hypnotist's suggestions, and therefore care must be taken to counteract any tendencies of the individual to attribute successes following the hypnosis to the treatment and the hypnotist rather than to himself.

In this regard I recall an interesting article in *Sport* magazine by Marty Bell, then an editor of the magazine, that richly dramatizes the dependency an athlete can develop in this area. According to Bell, Ken Norton's camp decided that their fighter did not need hypnosis to prepare for a second fight with Muhammad Ali. Unfortunately Norton, while perhaps convinced of this on an intellectual level, did not believe it emotionally. The result of this conflict inside Norton, according to Bell, was that the fighter lost his confidence before he entered the ring for the second fight. He was literally unable to keep his hands up, and even though Ali did not fight a particularly good fight, Norton lost.

This illustrates both one of the major uses of hypnosis and one of the major problems. The attitude of an athlete is crucial to his performance—a positive self-concept and confidence in one's own abilities are critical if performance is to be optimal. Coaches have long recognized this and in various ways have stressed the power of positive thinking to their athletes. Unfortunately, however, many athletes seem unable to believe in their own abilities, and their experience shows us that the harder they try to develop a positive attitude, the less they believe—and the more frustrated they become. When this occurs, it's practically impossible for them to effectively change their thoughts and feelings because they no longer have faith in their own ability to do so.

For the athlete with such a lack of self-confidence, hypnosis may be a useful preliminary tool. The hypnotist assumes responsibility for the athlete, and although the individual cannot place faith in himself, he does believe in the power of the hypnotist. This faith allows him to follow instructions, to relax, and to concentrate on those elements which will improve performance. However, for the growth of the athlete, the hypnotist must gradually be able to transfer the confidence placed in him back to the individual and into his own abilities. Then the athlete can do things for himself, as we will see in the following chapters.

Chapter Seven. **Self-Induced Relaxation Procedures**

Let me begin this section of the book with both a promise and a warning. First the promise. The training procedures to be presented in this and subsequent chapters *can* be used in a conscientiously applied program to greatly improve the quality and consistency of athletic performance. They are not magic, however. Thus the warning. The concept of some quickie solution to a problem, though it sells books and sounds exciting, is simply not a reality. Many times, following the initiation of relaxation training or meditation, some rather dramatic changes do occur within a short period of time. All too frequently, when this occurs, the athletes think they have accomplished their goal of learning to relax and they stop practicing the procedures. The usual result is a rapid regression back to where they were before they started—and an accompanying loss of confidence in the procedures themselves. Beware of miracle cures—all too often they evaporate.

As an example of the temporary miracle, I taught a golfer experiencing trouble with his putting the relaxation procedures we will be discussing here. He had been averaging about forty-two putts per eighteen holes. The next two rounds, after starting the procedures, he got down to thirty and thirty-two putts respectively. He was ecstatic, and assuming that he now had his problem under control, he stopped practicing the procedures. Over the next few rounds of golf he watched grimly as the number of putts climbed back up to a figure well over forty.

I also recall a talk I gave to a large audience on learning to gain control over anxiety and arousal. As part of the lecture I led them through the relaxation procedures presented in this chapter and then described to them all the marvelous improvements in level and consistency of performance and in feelings of self-worth that they could experience if they would practice these simple procedures twice a day for a few minutes. To my way of thinking, it was asking very little of them to achieve so much. After the talk, a hand went up and a well-spoken woman asked, "But what if I don't want to put out the effort required? Isn't there another way?" In a decidedly hostile voice, which I later regretted, I replied, "Yes! Just take fifteen milligrams of Valium."

The woman's question, however, was an honest one and not at all facetious. She was looking for results without work and she lacked the discipline and strength to assume responsibility for those results.

Now, having hopefully prepared you for the fact that you must work to gain control over yourself, let me introduce some specific relaxation training procedures. In particular this chapter focuses on procedures you can use to teach yourself to relax. Whereas hypnosis demands the presence of another person, you can do all the exercises presented here by yourself.

There are several immediate advantages to this. First the dependency problems which occasionally develop with the use of hypnosis are avoided. Then, too, you can avoid the expense and inconvenience of having to hire a hypnotist. Because hypnosis really should require the presence of an expert, its use is often limited to crisis situations or else to the treatment of important specific problems. In any case it's simply too expensive to retain a hypnotist on any kind of long-term basis. Finally, since these procedures are under your own control, you have them available to you at all times. For this reason alone, the potential benefits and applications cover a much broader area of possible improvement.

Autogenic Training

Progressive relaxation procedures were developed by Doctor Johannes H. Schultz, a German physician, around the turn of the century. However, Schultz's book, *Autogenic Training*, written with Wolfgang Luthe, did not appear in the United States until 1959. As an enlightened physician Schultz was well aware of the multitude of negative effects which anxiety could have on his patients' physical wellbeing. In an attempt to cope with these problems, he began using a variety of hypnotic techniques to reduce his patients' levels of anxiety. Over a period of years he realized that most of his patients seemed to report similar experiences, even though they were responding to different hypnotic techniques and individualized suggestions. Their descriptions of their feelings and the bodily changes experienced seemed constant and always followed a particular pattern. It was through the discovery of this shared experience that Schultz eventually developed the standard autogenic exercises.

A subject who wishes to learn to relax is taught to develop in succession: (1) feelings of heaviness in his arms and legs, (2) feelings of warmth in his arms and legs (the way his body feels after a good meal), (3) cardiac control and regulation, (4) control of respiration, (5) warmth in his abdomen, and (6) a cooler forehead.

To achieve these feelings, the subject practices the following exercises three times a day. On the first day the subject passively concentrates on heaviness in his dominant arm (right arm, if right-handed) from sixty to ninety seconds. He either sits or lies quietly with his eyes closed and silently keeps repeating to himself, "My right arm is heavy, I am at peace. . . ." Then the subject stretches his arm muscles on the count of one, takes a deep breath on the count of two, and opens his eyes on the count of three. One minute later he repeats the same procedure. The subject enacts three of these 60–90-second passive concentration periods in each training session and undertakes two training sessions a day. Once the subject is successful in developing the feeling of heaviness in his right arm, he moves to the left arm. When he can rapidly relax both arms within a 60–90-second period, he repeats the procedures with his legs. Then on to other parts of the body. At the end of about four months, he can go through all the standard exercises within ninety seconds. The subject sits down, closing his eyes, and begins thinking something like this: "My arms and legs are heavy and warm, my heartbeat is calm and regular, my breathing is deep and slow, my solar plexus is warm, my forehead is cool."

Once a person has mastered the standard exercises, he can begin to induce the same feelings under more stressful conditions. A goal that many practitioners successfully attain is to relax themselves completely in just a few seconds under stressful conditions. Athletes who are experienced autogenic practitioners report elimination of nervousness, increased relaxation, better technical control, improved relations with friends and teammates, and other beneficial effects. Moreover, articles and reports in athletic and scientific journals confirm the improvement autogenic training has helped athletes achieve in a wide variety of sports, including judo, golf, baseball, cycling, hockey, skiing, diving, tennis, and track.[1]

Variations in Relaxation Procedures

Many variations of autogenic training have been developed in both Europe and the United States. Generally modifications involve changes in the verbal formulas that are used (e.g., "My right arm is filled with sawdust" versus "My right arm is heavy and warm") and changes in the length of time subjects practice. For instance, in one program the athlete focuses from the start on all major muscle groups in succession—right arm, left arm, right leg, etc. To do this, the procedures are extended from 30–60 seconds to 15–30 minutes. By and large, however, these variations in the relaxation procedures seem to be more a matter of individual preference than of substantive difference. But whatever the technique, results can be dramatic.

In 1967 a shot putter came to me because he couldn't exceed his best mark of the previous year, even though he felt physically stronger. This athlete, despite his small size, held the conference record, but most of the coaches felt he had already reached—indeed exceeded—his potential.

For starters, I explained to the shot putter about the anxiety that accompanies competition and about the increased muscle tension that can result in the neck and shoulders. Even a small amount of tension in these muscles would be antagonistic to putting the shot. Accordingly I instructed him in the relaxation procedures he was to practice twice a day. Within the next four weeks he had two meets and he broke his own conference record each time out.

Another time I had the opportunity to coach a team of young divers, ranging in age from six to seven and in ability from beginners to state class. Pool time was limited, and this became a special problem when individuals were requested to try a dive which frightened them. These divers stood on the end of the board for several minutes trying to get up the courage to jump. Now if each of twenty kids spends five minutes thinking about a dive, not much diving gets done. To alleviate this problem, I started taking fifteen minutes of practice time and using it for relaxation training. I had the divers lie down on the pool deck, close their eyes, and then I talked them through a progressive relaxation exercise. Once they were relaxed, I had them rehearse the dive they were working on and I instructed them to think through the dive prior to getting on the board. I also told them that as soon as they actually got on the board, they were to come to attention, take a deep breath, and then execute the dive. They were told that all their mental preparation should occur before coming to attention on the board.

As a result of this training, my young divers spent far less time fidgeting on the board. They were more orderly, and there was less horsing around in line because they were busy getting ready mentally for their next turn. They enjoyed the procedures and exhibited less fear when asked to attempt new or difficult dives. And as a team this group went from fifth in a ten-team league to first in a single year.

Below I have outlined some relaxation procedures I've used with a number of athletes in different sports. These exercises, modified from procedures used by Dr. J. Wolpe,[2] encompass only about half the procedures that I use to get athletes psychologically ready. The exercises are designed to reduce tension, to improve the athlete's ability to concentrate (to control and direct attention), and to teach him to recognize and counteract increasing tension before it gets out of hand.

My own practice has been to meet with athletes once a week for four weeks. At the first meeting I discuss the importance of relaxation and then take them through the exercises. At the end of this session I answer questions, talk about feelings they might have had while going through the exercises, and instruct them to practice the procedures twice a day for ten to fifteen minutes at a time. They are instructed to pick a time and place for practice where they will not be disturbed and where distracting stimuli will be kept to a minimum. They are told to silently go over the procedures in their mind. It is very important that their concentration during these practices be passive—that is, they must not fight to develop the various feelings. They will find their thoughts wandering to other things, and when this occurs, they should not become upset. Instead they must passively respond to the distraction by simply recognizing that their attention has wandered and by redirecting it to the exercises. Even if they are distracted a large number of times in a session, each time their response should be, "Oh, my attention wandered—that's all right, now back to the exercise."

The next three sessions are used to make sure practice is proceeding properly and to make any adjustments in the procedures which seem necessary. Often these sessions are important for keeping the individuals motivated and for building their confidence in the exercises and in themselves. During the week they are asked to keep a record of their practice and to evaluate their success each time by rating the depth of their relaxation as well as their ability to rehearse. (Table 7.1 is a copy of the form that they use to keep track of their progress.)

I always try to emphasize that at first, learning to relax will be difficult and that in fact several sessions may pass before relaxation begins to develop. Even if the feelings do not develop in particular sessions, the individual is instructed not to spend more than fifteen minutes in passive concentration. To continue to try to relax when it isn't happening can be very frustrating and often increases tension rather than reducing it.

Table 7.1   Relaxation Record

Relaxation Scale
1. Unable to relax 2. Mild relaxation 3. Moderately relaxed 4. Very relaxed 5. Completely relaxed

Rehearsal Scale
1. Unable to visualize or develop kinesthetic recall (imagery and bodily feelings) 2. 3. Fair visual recall of bodily sensations 4. 5. Complete recall

Session Number

Relaxation	1	2	3	4	5	6	7	8	9	10	11	12	13	14
a.m.														
p.m.														
	15	16	17	18	19	20	21	22	23					
a.m.														
p.m.														
Rehearsal	1	2	3	4	5	6	7	8	9	10	11	12	13	14
a.m.														
p.m.														
	15	16	17	18	19	20	21	22	23					
a.m.														
p.m.														

As with hypnosis it may be useful initially to put the following procedures on tape. Once the general format is learned, however, it would be better to think them through rather than to rely on the tape. In addition, with experience you will find relaxation will develop much more quickly. When this occurs, the relaxation instructions should be shortened to accommodate this. Remember, the ultimate goal is to learn to relax completely in just a few seconds.

Relaxation Procedures

These procedures should be practiced twice a day for about ten minutes at a time (evenings are often a good time to practice). The order of the steps involved is very important; however, the particular words or thoughts that the athlete uses to accomplish each step are not. For example, it is important that you relax prior to concentrating on bowling. When you are concentrating on relaxing your arms, we don't care if you say to yourself, "Now I am going to release all the muscular tension in my hands, fingers, and forearms," or if you say, "Now I am going to relax the muscles in my hands, fingers, and arms."

Prior to beginning the exercise, find a quiet, comfortable place where you will not be disturbed and where you can either sit or lie down. If you wear contact lenses, you may want to remove them. If you have on restrictive clothing (like a tie), you may want to loosen it. Make yourself comfortable with your hands at your sides or in your lap and you are ready to begin.

1. Close your eyes and take three deep breaths, inhaling and exhaling deeply and slowly. *As you exhale, relax your entire body as much as you can. Continue to notice your breathing throughout the session. You will find that as you exhale, your relaxation will become deeper.*

2. *Now clench both of your fists. Close them and squeeze them tighter and tighter together. As you squeeze them, notice the tension in your forearms, your hands, and your fingers. That's fine, now let them go, relax them. Let your fingers become loose and notice the pleasant feeling of heaviness in your arms and hands as the tension disappears. Feel the heaviness of your arms and hands as they rest against your body or the chair. That's fine, try it one more time, clench both fists and feel the tension, squeeze harder, hold the tension, now let go and completely relax.*

3. *Now bend your elbows, clench your fists, and flex your biceps. Flex them harder, hold the tension and study it. Now unbend your elbows, relax your hands, get your arms back in a comfortable position, study how your arms feel as you completely let go and relax them.*

4. *Now straighten your arms and flex the triceps muscle in the back of your upper arms. Hold the tension, increase it, squeeze harder, study the tension. That's fine, now relax, return your arms to a comfortable position and enjoy the release from the tension. Enjoy the feelings, and even when you feel completely relaxed, try and let go even more.*

5. *Now clench your teeth, feel the muscles tightening in your neck and jaws. Once again, study the tension, clench your teeth tighter, tighter. Now relax your jaws, let your mouth open slightly, and feel your muscles loosen, feel the relief from the tension.*

6. *Pay attention to your neck muscles. Press your head back as far as it will go and feel the tension, now roll it straight to the right. Again feel the increase in the tension in your muscles. Move your head to the left, pressing hard and feeling the tension in your muscles. Hold the same position and study the tension. Now let your*

head move into a comfortable position and relax the muscles in your neck and shoulders. Notice the pleasant change as you feel the tension leaving your muscles. Pay attention to how your neck and shoulders feel when the muscles are relaxed.

7. *Now pay attention to your breathing and relax your entire body. Breathe deeply and slowly, and as you exhale, relax all the muscles in your arms. Just let yourself go and completely relax. Let your mouth open slightly and relax the muscles in your face, jaw, and forehead. Relax the muscles in your neck and shoulders. . . . Relax the muscles in your feet, your calves, and your thighs. . . . That's fine. . . . Just completely relax and let yourself go. Continue to breathe deeply and slowly, and enjoy the pleasant feeling of being completely relaxed.*

8. *At this time those of you who wish may practice rehearsing the sights and feelings that you associate with a particular pleasant activity. This practice should not last for more than four to five minutes.*

9. *Now, since you have relaxed so completely, it is best to take your time in moving around. Get out of this relaxed state by using three steps. First, count one and take a deep breath and hold it. Second, count two and stretch your arms and legs, then exhale. Third, count three and open your eyes. You should be wide awake and feeling very relaxed and comfortable.*

Procedure Summary

1. *Close your eyes and breathe deeply and slowly.*
2. *Relax the muscles in your forearms.*
3. *Relax your biceps.*
4. *Relax your triceps.*
5. *Relax your face, jaw, and forehead.*

6. *Relax your neck and shoulders.*
7. *Breathe slowly and relax your entire body.*
8. *Rehearse an activity.*
9. *Take a deep breath, stretch, and open your eyes.*

One method of shortening the procedures is to drop out the tensing of various muscle groups. The rationale behind tensing and then relaxing your muscles, as given in the relaxation procedures, is that this allows you to learn to differentiate feelings of tension from those associated with being relaxed. It was mentioned earlier that many individuals are not aware of increasing tension until it is too late to do anything about it. These procedures can sensitize you to those feelings and in so doing improve your ability to control tension better. Once this awareness is gained, therefore, you no longer need to include the tensing of muscles in your relaxation training. To do so becomes a waste of time, acting only to prolong the induction of a relaxed state. Ultimately you should reach the point of being able to relax completely in the time it takes you to *take a deep breath, inhaling deeply* and *exhaling slowly.* As you are exhaling, you mentally direct your attention by thinking, "My arms and legs are heavy and completely relaxed, and I am at ease." Soon you will find that within the space of one or two breaths you will be completely relaxed.

The procedures as I have presented them focus on just a few muscle groups. Athletes in various sports may wish to add others or to concentrate more heavily on specific areas. Divers and gymnasts may want to emphasize relaxation of neck and shoulder muscles. In contrast, golfers may be interested in developing a better feeling for the muscular tension in their hips, waist, and back. Improved awareness in these areas result in a better feel for the swing and the position of the hips as contact is made with the ball. Depending on the individual's needs, instructions to focus on these muscle groups can be introduced any time after focusing on the feelings in the arms and legs.

Some of the advantages in using these procedures, as opposed to hypnosis, have already been discussed, but let's summarize them.

First, in contrast to the small percentage of the population that is susceptible to hypnosis, research indicates that about forty-five per cent of the athletes who try these procedures are able to benefit from them.[3] There is no dependency on another individual. Another advantage is that the relaxation procedures have broader and more flexible applications. The individual is free to apply them whenever and wherever he wants. And certainly they are far less costly to the athlete, since much less professional time is involved.

Having said that, let me finish up this chapter by pointing out a few problems which may arise in the use of these procedures.

Athletes tend to be active rather than passive, and for some individuals it's a very difficult task, particularly at first, just to sit and relax. In addition, self-directed procedures work only as long as the individuals have faith in their own ability to employ them. Early in training it's difficult for many athletes to maintain this confidence. When this occurs, motivation to practice drops off, doubts continue to build, and the athletes may give up.

Of more importance, those individuals who have a fairly delicately balanced biochemistry or those who take medication for any hypertensive or endocrine disorder should not undertake this regimen without their physician's go-ahead. The reason for this caution is simple. As the relaxation training begins to work, tension decreases and the need for tension-related medication also goes down. Unless some process is available for altering medication in conjunction with training, the individual could unwittingly overdose himself. One startling example: relaxation training has lowered the amount of insulin required by a diabetic from eighty to thirty units a day.

Chapter Eight. **Transcendental Meditation**

In the last few years Eastern meditation procedures based on the Hindu discipline of yoga have received a great deal of publicity in the United States. In particular the discipline known as transcendental meditation (TM) has attracted hundreds of thousands of practitioners. TM, according to its proponents, is supposed to rejuvenate and normalize the function of the nervous system, eliminate mental stress, promote clear thinking and comprehension, enrich perception, and eliminate discord. From the perspective of the physiological changes which have been found to be associated with the practice of TM, it does appear to closely resemble the procedures we've just discussed, autogenic training and progressive relaxation.[1]

TM was first given prominence in this country in the 1960s when the famous British rock group, the Beatles, went to India to study with the founder of the movement, the Maharishi Mahesh Yogi. Since then there have been bestselling books on the subject, and TM centers have popped up in most major cities in the United States to educate the converts and convert the uneducated. Late in

1975 the Indian government, spurred by the wide interest in both yoga and TM in many Western countries, announced the results of a three-year research program set up to study the actual therapeutic applications of these practices. A team of physicians and medical researchers at the medical institute of Benares Hindu University found, the government reported, that yoga and meditation was useful in providing relief from a variety of the so-called stress diseases so prevalent in industrial countries. These included high blood pressure, peptic ulcer, heart disease, insomnia, and drug addiction. According to the head of the research program, Doctor K. N. Udupa, the following were among the physiological and psychological improvements registered by patients: loss of excess weight, reduction of nervous tension and mental unrest, improved appetites, reduction of respiratory problems, and a lowering of high blood pressure and cholesterol levels.

If this research is substantiated in the West, we can expect continued growth of interest in yoga and TM, which will be both a positive thing—we already know TM has benefits—and an extension of an existing problem. The TM centers spreading throughout this country are usually staffed by instructors who have "met the requirements of the Maharishi himself." Moreover, TM instructorships are similar to fast food and ice cream franchises in that instructors go through a training program, become certified instructors themselves, and then teach others for a fee. The fees are being raised, but at this writing they are around $175 for four sessions (about one hour each) and climbing. These fees are shared between the instructor and a central administrative organization that takes care of publicity, training facilities, etc.

The inevitable result of such a system is that many instructors become little more than pressure salesmen trying to make a buck and making promises that they can't keep. I repeat, my statements on this issue are not meant as an indictment of TM since I am convinced of its usefulness, but there *is* reason for concern here. My concern is with misrepresentation in the form of false promises or misinformation or simply the exaggeration of some finding. These things may result from overzealousness on the part of instructors or they may be a direct result of good old greed. In fact, given the large number of people involved in TM, it is amazing that the organization controls its representatives as well as it does.

On other grounds as well, some caution needs to be exercised by an individual who plans on using TM. As with the other techniques we've discussed, TM is not a magical no-work solution to stress. It *can* help you gain some control over attentional processes, anxiety, and physiological arousal, but *you* must work at it for that to happen. In addition, there is no convincing evidence to suggest that it offers any more than many other relaxation procedures.

Practice Sessions

During the first TM session, subjects are usually told what physiological and psychological changes occur as a consequence of the meditation procedure. Following this, an instructor selects a mantra that is appropriate for the subject. The mantra is simply a sound; for instance, the nonsense syllable *Om* (Ahhōm) has been a popular mantra.

Once the subject has been given a mantra, he is instructed to "perceive" it—"passively concentrate" on it—twice a day for fifteen to twenty minutes. During these sessions he sits quietly with his eyes closed. Without forcing attention on the mantra, he simply lets himself—in the

most literal sense—experience it. In this way his thoughts
are free to rise to a "more creative level." If he finds himself
emotionally disturbed or if he becomes aware of distractions, he responds to them in a passive way—simply
reflecting what's occurring—and lets his mind return to
experiencing the mantra.

This passive reflection procedure is critical and it's a
common element in many meditation procedures other
than TM. It is essentially the same type of concentration
used in many forms of hypnotic induction, autogenic training, and progressive relaxation. The idea behind passive
reflection is that the subject does not try to exert control
over his attention. He inevitably finds himself distracted
when this occurs, and as he becomes aware of it ("Oops, my
mind wandered"), he doesn't order but *lets* his thoughts
return to the mantra. It's important to note that this process involves the relaxation of control over thought processes in terms of (1) not forcing attention and (2) allowing
the mind to wander. And when distraction of attention does
occur, as it will, it involves simply reminding (*not* forcing)
yourself to think of (focus on) the mantra—which is a neutral, nonarousing stimulus.

After the initial session in which the subject receives his
mantra, he is required to return three more times, usually
on successive days, so that the instructor can ascertain
whether or not the subject is practicing correctly. After
these four sessions the subject is strictly on his own.

Physiological Effects of Meditation

There has been some fairly good research conducted on the
physiological effects of TM. The most well-known study to
date was reported in *Scientific American* in February 1972.

The research was conducted by Dr. Herbert Benson, a Harvard Medical School cardiologist, and by Dr. Robert Wallace, a research physiologist. Their research indicates the following physiological responses following TM exercises: lowering of blood pressure, a slowing of respiration and heart rate, and an increase in alpha activity in the brain. In addition, both oxygen consumption and blood lactate levels decreased markedly.

The changes that Wallace and Benson describe are of particular interest to athletes. For example, the rapid reduction of blood lactate levels indicates that meditation facilitates recovery from stress and fatigue. In brief, this is a *very promising* research area.

Applications of TM to Athletics

Currently a number of professional athletes employ TM procedures in their training. Several UCLA basketball players, including Bill Walton, and ex-Olympic diver Craig Lincoln have also employed TM. Recently the American Foundation for the Science of Creative Intelligence (the organization responsible for the development and spread of TM in the United States), recognizing the applicability of TM procedures to athletics, formed a special division to further this development.

To be honest, it's still too early to evaluate the effects of these procedures on athletic achievement in any controlled scientific fashion. However, athletes using these procedures are firm in their belief that they feel better, learn faster, are more relaxed, and have more energy than ever before.

As I noted earlier, we do know that there is a remarkable

similarity in the physiological changes that occur in persons practicing TM and the various forms of autogenic training. At present there is no scientific explanation for this, but my own belief and one shared by Dr. Benson is that the passive-reflective type of attention which individuals develop under these procedures accounts for these similar physiological changes (see Dr. Benson's *The Relaxation Response*).

Passive-Reflective Attention

Through his practicing to develop a passive attention, the subject eventually learns to avoid becoming trapped in negative, anxiety-inducing thoughts, which are also the type of thoughts that feed on each other—for example, "I'm tired, I can't go on, I'm going to lose." This ability to avoid emotional traps is most valuable because it helps keep anxiety down, allows for a quick recovery from stress since the body is able to relax, and allows the subject to maintain control over attentional processes.

It surely comes as no surprise to you that painful thoughts and imagined threats can induce significant physiological changes in us. You only need to think of some of your own nightmares or childhood reactions to scary movies to realize that your thoughts can and do create some disturbing physiological experiences—you wake up screaming, in a cold sweat, with your heart racing. You're so scared you can't move—you're sure someone's in the room. For that matter a frightening cycle of thoughts and feelings often leads to physical changes and increases in arousal of which you may be unaware at first—then, when you feel your heart beating faster or have difficulty swallowing or feel slightly dizzy, you become more frightened still. Thus the cycle of more arousal and more fear continues. Your attention becomes narrowed and focused in a negative way, directed inward toward your physical reactions to the stress.

Obviously enough, the situation is a negative one. It's possible, however, to learn to develop a positive set. When negative sets are broken, it's usually because some strong outside source, such as the hypnotist or the coach in Chapter 7, has distracted you. This kind of distraction allows you to calm down without being consciously aware of it. It's like falling asleep at night. If you're trying to fall asleep, you fail. Eventually you become distracted, your thoughts begin drifting out of control, and finally you fall asleep. In the same way, when you're emotionally upset, your attention must first be directed away from your feelings and fears. When this happens, you become aware of the fact that you are no longer upset.

Since most of us, without the appropriate training, are unable to control our attentional processes and most assuredly are unaware of how they affect us, the ability to concentrate passively, to reflect, is something we have to learn. For instance, a good night's sleep allows some physiological recovery, but it doesn't help with emotional problems. We're trapped in our emotional feelings even in sleep, as our dreams reveal so vividly, but those individuals who have learned to concentrate passively claim that their sleep improves as a result of this training.

Generally speaking, the application of TM procedures is similar to that of progressive relaxation and autogenic training. One major difference is that the procedures, *at least as practiced by TM instructors,* are conceptually more difficult to integrate with the other procedures discussed in this book. This is due to the emphasis that TM training places on maintaining a passive-reflective (noncompetitive) attitude. The implication is that there is no place during the meditation procedure, or following it, for controlling and focusing attention, but this is simply not true. In fact the relaxation which can develop through TM and/or other procedures can definitely be used to prepare the person for effective focusing of attention—as we will see in the next chapter.

Exactly how does TM function in athletics? Well, TM procedures can be helpful in improving an athlete's general feeling of well-being as well as increasing his energy level and his ability to concentrate. In particular they are very useful to athletes who engage in endurance events which require little in the way of external attention—events such as the distance events in track and swimming. Theoretically an athlete's ability to perceive the mantra in meditation—in other words, his ability to maintain a passive-reflective attitude—keeps him from becoming locked into negative, self-defeating thoughts and feelings. By being able to avoid focusing attention on how tired or sore he is, he can avoid increasing tension, and this results in an increase in endurance.

However, TM procedures are probably most applicable in those competitive situations where an athlete's responses require no thought, where movements have been learned so well that they have become automatic. Because of their emphasis on passive concentration, TM procedures may help you perform in those situations where you are not concentrating on the act but are simply *being* the act. For example, complicated gymnastics routines or dives are often practiced to the point where they are almost reflexive. In fact they sometimes become so automatic that we lose our feel for them and are unable to tell when we make a mistake. This lack of awareness makes it almost impossible for us to modify a move once it is learned because as soon as we have to think about what we are doing, the whole routine falls apart. Even some of the sports which demand that we react to the moves of opponents can be developed to the point where little if any thought is required on our part. A certain punch by an opponent always leads to our making the same block and counterpunch.

It would be absurd to say that you should never think during competition. However, the major downfall for many of us is that we think too much. When this happens, it is because we are so eager to anticipate what our opponent will do that we lose awareness of what is actually going on. This type of mistake is responsible for an end dropping the pass because he is thinking of running for the goal line before he catches the ball, or a tennis player who misjudges a lob because she's thinking about where she will place her return. If you have a tendency to respond in this way, some modification of a TM procedure could be very helpful to you.

Meditation in Tennis

Not too long ago I had a nationally ranked female tennis player come to me for some help. If things started going poorly for her early in a match, she said, she became overly concerned and lost control of herself. Not surprisingly, she became furious over her mistakes, and this anger led to an additional increase in muscle tension and to corresponding deterioration in her play. To counteract this process, I instructed her to concentrate on the tennis ball so intently that she would see it even when it was covered by her opponent's hand. I told her to distinguish the fuzz on it, notice the spin, and in fact watch it so closely that she could see it dent the strings on her racquet when she hit it. I pointed out that she did not need to think about her shots—she already knew them so well that they had become automatic. All the concentration she needed was encompassed by the ball. Everything depended on her watching the ball.

Before she started this procedure, however, I warned her that at first she would actually find it impossible to concentrate on the ball in this way and that she would find herself becoming angry and frustrated at her failure to do so. I told her that this was precisely what I wanted to happen. Each time her mind wandered, she would have to direct her attention back to the ball, and the more practice she would get at developing a passive-reflective focus. Each time that she found herself distracted she was to say, "That's all right, back to the ball." In effect I was asking her to use the ball in much the same way a meditator uses a mantra.

Within a week she began reporting that she would find herself slipping into a trance. She would lose awareness of everything except the ball and as a result found herself feeling more relaxed and getting to shots she previously wouldn't have believed she could reach. She also mentioned that occasionally she would become excited by the realization that she had been in a trance, but when this occurred, she simply said, "That's all right, back to the ball."

Applications of TM procedures like this one could be useful in many sports where the development of a rhythm or focus on a single object, such as the ball, is appropriate.

It must be emphasized, however, that such a focus implies that you do not need to think about what you are going to do when that ball comes at you.

Problems in Using TM Procedures

TM can be difficult for some athletes because they equate the procedures with an adherence to specific religious or mystical beliefs. This problem is heightened by the terminology and methods TM instructors use to communicate with the student. For example, the magical-mystical aspect is dramatized by the secrecy that surrounds the mantra assigned to an individual. Prior to receiving the special mantra (suited to and chosen for your age and personality), the individual is told never to reveal it to others. Advertisements for TM often take the form of a religious movement—for example, the "year of action for the world plan." This approach to selling TM obviously attracts many individuals, but it also serves to keep away others who might benefit from the training.

In addition, the idea of simply sitting and thinking about a sound for twenty minutes twice a day is about as appealing as a bowl full of spinach. Many athletes in particular have a great deal of difficulty sitting still for any period of time. Fortunately, however, there are other procedures available which can be used to teach the development of a passive type of concentration.

Active Meditation

The Oriental martial arts aikido, tai-chi, and tai-kwan-do can be practiced in a way that trains an athlete to develop passive concentration. One way to understand this concept is to view your own body as your mantra. You learn to passively experience the movements and feelings of your body. If you become distracted, you simply accept the distraction and return attention to the immediate feelings that the movement of your body creates as you exercise.

If you engage in sports such as tennis, crew, swimming, gymnastics, basketball, or any sport which requires you to maintain motion over a period of time, you have probably experienced this moving meditation. On these occasions you lose awareness of yourself for a while, only later realizing that you have been completely absorbed in your bodily feelings as you moved through space. There is no reason why you cannot, through practice, increase the frequency of this experience as you let your own particular sport become your mantra.

Because of the energy expenditure required by this physical activity, it's doubtful that the same physiological changes occur from this active meditation as from the more passive forms. Athletes report, however, that when they play under these conditions, they do feel less fatigued and need to expend less energy.

It should be pointed out at this juncture that passive concentration, although it is one of the major advantages of meditation, is also limited in that this type of attentional focus is inappropriate when you must concentrate on learning a new skill or on executing moves which you have not attempted before. For example, one of the things that the tennis player I worked with hoped to achieve, once her game became more consistent, was to get more power in her forehand. If she maintained a meditative type of attention, she would have been unable to develop this aspect of her game. Her responses with a meditative focus would be automatic. Thus her stroke would be very consistent, but it would be the same stroke she had been using in the past. To increase her power, it was necessary for her to concentrate her attention on such cues as her own muscle tension, the sound and feel of the ball hitting her racquet, and the feeling of her arm moving through the air. Her learning to hit with more power required an ongoing analysis of what she was doing, but this could be disruptive in competition because it would interfere with her ability to maintain a constant awareness of the ball. However, the focus was necessary in practice because she wished to alter her existing style.

Obviously the ability and necessity to maintain a passive attentional focus must depend on your current level of skill and on what you are trying to achieve. If you know the sport well, a passive type of concentration is ideal. If you are just learning or if you are trying to improve an existing skill, then an active attentional focus is required.

Blending an Active and Passive Attention

Most often you will find yourself trying to move between the active and passive types of attention. In most sports there are times when an active focus would be helpful—say, between points in a tennis game or between pitches in a baseball game. Some athletes are quite capable of effectively using these pauses to think about the game and to plan strategies. Other athletes, however, have a great deal of difficulty trying to use this time. Once they start to think between points, they find themselves unable to break away from those thoughts. They become trapped inside their own heads and don't get back to the game as quickly as they should. Anxiety has much to do with this particular problem, and to a certain extent, learning to relax helps overcome it. If your tendency is to become trapped in your thoughts, then it is important for you to maintain a passive focus even between points. Indeed, for some athletes, particularly highly competitive ones, it is often necessary for them to wait until a game or match is completely over before attempting to analyze their play.

I think that Billie Jean King is a good example of an athlete who has control over her attentional processes. Between points she talks to herself, reviews a missed shot, and psychs herself up, but as soon as she sets up to receive or to serve, her concentration is back on the ball. Unfortunately, few athletes have the demonstrated ability to concentrate like Billie Jean, but this ability can be developed and improved.

As more control is gained over attention, the ability to think during competition increases. We all need to know our own limits. This can be accomplished only by first learning to recognize when our thoughts are interfering with our performance and creating tension. Practice in meditation or relaxation procedures as well as mental rehearsal procedures, which are discussed in the next chapter, can be used very successfully to increase this awareness.

Chapter Nine. Mental Rehearsal

Mental rehearsal, as I am applying the term to competitive athletics, refers to your systematically thinking about your performance in some past or future athletic endeavor. Rehearsal, I know, would seem to be directed to future endeavors, but thinking about how you *have* played obviously has something to do with how you hope you *will* play.

Many athletes use mental rehearsal procedures as a means of increasing their learning speed and improving their performance. Basketball star Pete Maravich has said that he mentally replays entire games in his head. Eastern European gymnastics and diving coaches will often have their team members mentally rehearse an entire series of moves prior to competition. Weight lifters mentally picture their lift just before the actual attempt. In fact there is hardly a sport where athletes haven't attempted either to rehearse mentally what they are about to do or to analyze what they have already done.

In spite of the fairly common application of various types of rehearsal procedures across sports, relatively little has been done scientifically to examine the effects of these practices on different athletes. Some athletes appear to have found the procedures extremely helpful, but others have not been able to use them effectively and have even found that they interfere with performance. It's thought that the failure of some athletes to use these procedures effectively is most likely due to their inappropriate application rather than to the procedures themselves. This chapter presents a description of how rehearsal techniques can be helpful in competition. In addition I've tried to provide you with a strategy for deciding what type of rehearsal procedure will be most helpful in a particular situation.

What Is Mental Rehearsal?

When I mention the subject of mental rehearsal, many individuals immediately think of a person quietly imagining that he is watching a motion picture of himself. It's as though the individual rehearsing is equipped with a camera in his head and has been taking pictures of himself as he engages in athletic activity. Unfortunately very few athletes do develop this ability to visualize activities in such a clear and complete way. Some people picture blurred images while others, instead of seeing a movie, picture a series of still snapshots. For example, a pole vaulter might get a picture of what his body position looks like as he starts to take his first step at the top of the runway; the second picture may be of himself in full stride; the third, as he is planting the pole; the fourth, as his legs begin to come up past his head; etc. For this athlete all the activity which occurs between these snapshots is omitted. He is rehearsing his feelings and movements at a few critical junctures rather than the entire process.

In addition to rehearsing through the use of visual imagery, most athletes can also recall and rehearse the kinesthetic cues (body feelings) which accompany the activity. In fact it is particularly important to be able to develop the bodily sensations which accompany a given activity. Then, too, not only can the visual and kinesthetic cues be recalled, but so can the sensations of sound and smell. Everything from the roar of the engines in racing, the grunts and shouts in football, and the sound of skis moving through icy snow, to the smell of sawdust, rosin, and popcorn can be recreated mentally.

Imagery versus Rehearsal

Attempts to use your ability to recall the various sensations associated with a sport in order to improve performance are not new. Visual images have often been used to facilitate an athlete's response to suggestions of all types. Along this line, coaches in Eastern European countries have used the visualization of particular scenes to help athletes develop the level of competitive tension that is appropriate for them. Thus those athletes who need to psych themselves up visualize themselves in and rehearse the competitive situation, while those who need to relax imagine some peaceful, calming scene.

Let me make a technical distinction here. There is a difference between mental rehearsal and simple imagery. By definition, rehearsal involves an active studying of an image or a series of images. The pole vaulter in the previous example rehearsed his movements in a logical fashion. By contrast, imagery simply involves the ability to develop an image without necessarily analyzing its content. The difference might be seen as acting in a movie as opposed to watching it. Simply watching is not enough since it does not often involve conscious attempts at control of attentional processes and tension levels. For instance, right now, without actually engaging in the movements, attempt to get both the image and the feelings associated with kicking a ball. Notice how, as you carefully attend to each movement, you begin to actually use the muscles involved. You don't use them in a way that increases strength but in a way that helps your coordination and timing.

Application of Rehearsal to Athletics

Visual and kinesthetic rehearsal have been used fairly extensively by coaches in gymnastics, swimming, and diving. Particularly in diving and gymnastics, there are points in time when the athlete has no idea of where in space his body is. On many dives, individuals are required to somersault and twist at the same time, and things happen so rapidly that it's impossible to think about the experience while it's occurring. Rehearsal procedures are often used, therefore, to assist these athletes in becoming aware of body position and movement through the recall of kinesthetic cues and the pairing of these with visual images.

Athletes have reported remarkable improvement with mental rehearsal. For example, within two weeks I had a bowler increase his average by twenty pins per game and a golfer decrease the number of strokes per round from an average of eighty-six for eighteen holes down to eighty. Although both these athletes are now firm believers in mental rehearsal, I have no way of proving that their improvements were due solely to the rehearsal procedures they employed. Obviously, as changes in performance began to occur, there were changes in their confidence as well.

Some of the controlled studies that have been conducted

in this area appear to indicate that mental rehearsal can be very effective, particularly for learning relatively simple motor skills. In fact one study found that mental practice at shooting free throws was as effective as actual practice in improving performance. The Russians and Czechs have examined the effects of mental rehearsal on more complex motor activities and have found it helpful there as well. In one study they compared equally skilled triple jumpers. Half the subjects memorized and rehearsed the entire sequence of movements in the triple jump, while this aspect of training was withheld from the other half of the subjects. At the end of training, those subjects who employed visualization were jumping farther than those who had not used the technique. A lot closer to home, I have had individuals attempt to increase the amount of weight they could bench-press through the use of rehearsal procedures, and they have had remarkable success. One individual was able to give a very clear, logical explanation for his increase of about forty pounds, and it did not involve strength. Through the rehearsal process he became aware that when he attempted a heavy lift, he arched his back too much, losing power. Simply by visualizing this mistake, he was able to correct it immediately and to increase his lifts dramatically.

These studies show how the subjects used visualization of performance as a means of improving their skill, but there are many ways in which rehearsal procedures can be used by athletes. Some other uses can be seen by recognizing the factors that seem to differentiate superior athletes from average ones.

First of all, top athletes have a better kinesthetic sense than ordinary ones. They can detect subtle differences in shape and weight that few other people pick up. In the same way they are very sensitive to the visual aspects of their environment. Earl Monroe, for example, can walk out on the basketball court and tell if the rim is a quarter of an inch off level. In addition, the really good athletes seem to automatically memorize information which is important. O. J. Simpson is so good at seeing the total field and instinctively reacting to positions and movements that his ability has been described by athletes and the press as extrasensory perception. Studies have shown that if a group of skiers walk to the top of a slalom course, the better skiers memorize the position of the gates, and many of them also visualize their body positions passing through the gates. Finally, the great athletes have a better feel for their bodies as they move through space. Tom Seaver, the Mets pitcher, and Mike Marshall of the Dodgers attribute much of their skill to an awareness of what their bodies are doing when they pitch. Seaver maintains that he doesn't have to think about it, he just feels himself pitch. What's especially interesting is that Seaver is convinced that most pitchers, even the star hurlers in the major leagues, do not have this awareness. Similarly, in my discussions with professional athletes, I have often been amazed by how little they knew about what their bodies felt like under different conditions. In a very real sense, they were unaware of what they were doing. To attain these skills, the ability to develop a broad-internal attentional focus is important.

The ability to use visual imagery as a method of memorizing a large amount of information has a special significance. Although language would seem to be the obvious tool for describing behavior and communicating to others, it can be a slow and laborious process. In many sports, events occur at tremendous speed, and if you had to use language to describe what was happening, you wouldn't be able to react quickly enough. As an example, imagine trying to talk to yourself about a hockey puck coming at your head at more than a hundred miles an hour. Or try to describe, in words, a dive as you're executing it. Imagine how many times you would be hit by Muhammad Ali in the time it takes you to think "Oh, oh, here comes his left jab."

Limiting What You Must Attend To

The limitations of language are obvious. In fact research by the Russians indicates that athletes during competition think in terms of images rather than words. This ability to use images and thus to recognize particular situations and enhance your ability to respond can be facilitated by rehearsal. In developing the ability to visualize situations, you'll find that you can more easily commit them to memory. Instead of memorizing a group of impressions and then using these to build a picture, you visualize the whole and then use the picture to remember the parts. This strategy is much more effective because in any situation there's a great deal of information that doesn't need to be processed in order to be remembered. Because you have observed similar situations in the past and know what is contained within them, you don't need to catalogue the elements. For example, if you quickly glance at a baseball diamond and someone then asks you to recall the positions of the players, you can probably do it quite easily—because you process only the information that's out of place. Instead of having to memorize the positions of the nine defensive players and the hitter, you notice only the one or two people out of position. Your knowledge of baseball automatically allows you to fill in the rest of the positions without having to attend to them consciously.

Through visual recall of various athletic situations, you

can train yourself to take the pictures of your environment that allow you to remember the gates in a slalom course or which club to select for a particular golf shot. In addition this rehearsal process helps you make a *discriminative cue analysis* of various athletic situations.

Discriminative Cues

It never ceases to amaze me that so many athletes do not know what they should be responding to in a particular situation. In any athletic situation, there are stimuli (discriminative cues) that are critical determinants of successful performance. The awareness of these crucial stimuli gives many athletes an advantage over others. Just what the critical cues are depends on the situation and on the skill of the athletes involved. As basic skills are developed and become reflexive, some of the cues which were important earlier no longer need to be attended to consciously. A child just learning to play baseball needs to pay conscious attention to the placement of his feet in the batter's box, to his grip on the bat, to his stance, to the position of his body, and so forth. An experienced hitter automatically assumes a batting stance, and it simply feels right. He doesn't have to check his grip on the bat—there's simply a total feeling, and once this feeling has developed, attentional processes are freed to focus on other things. For example, an experienced squash player doesn't have to wait to see the ball in flight to react. Like a good boxer or open-field tackler, he's able to anticipate his opponent's movements.

Obviously, there are cues which tell you what your opponent will do, and yet many times you cannot identify what they are. If you don't know what to react to at either the conscious or unconscious level—that is, if you can't make a discriminative cue analysis—chances are that you're only going to be an average athlete.

Conscious Awareness

Maury Wills used discriminative cues effectively the year he stole 104 bases for the Dodgers, and so did Lou Brock when he broke Wills's record in 1974. They both analyzed the moves of the various pitchers in the league and learned when the pitchers were about to throw to first or to the plate. Both men, by gradually enlarging their lead off the base and forcing the pitchers to throw, could systematically gain the information they needed to know in order to steal successfully. In effect Wills and Brock were creating situations in which they could perform discriminative cue analyses. By forcing the pitchers to respond in certain ways, they were able to learn which particular movements indicated that it was safe for them to steal.

Unconscious or Natural Responses

Unconscious examples of using discriminative cues occur all the time. When O.J. Simpson gained over 2000 yards in 1973, he was asked how he was able to pick his holes so well. He responded, "I don't think about it, I just run." This "it just comes natural" response is actually common among great athletes, and yet it doesn't really explain what happens.

As the Russian research indicates, athletes think in images during competition. We might imagine O.J. taking snapshots of his environment and responding "instinctively" to the positions of the players in the picture. This "instinctive" response is based on some real cues that successful experiences have taught O.J. to react to—without having to think about it, O.J. and other athletes have learned to recognize the important cues in a situation and ignore extraneous ones. O.J. doesn't bother to sit down after the game and figure out what it was that he responded to, and this prevents him from being able to verbalize what the discriminative cues are. With success, there is often little motivation to go back and analyze the situation. On the other hand, through the use of a mental rehearsal process that involves developing the athletes' awareness of discriminative cues (what to see and feel versus what to ignore), much of the luck surrounding performance can be removed. So let me give you an idea of the strategies I might use to help an athlete make that discriminative cue analysis.

Discriminative Cues Indicating Increases in Tension

A college coach referred one of his basketball players to me quite early in the season. The player was shooting fouls badly and had made only two of ten attempts in an important game. Understandably the coach was upset, because the previous year this athlete had averaged eighty per cent of his free throws. In response to the player's bad start, the coach immediately began to change the player's shot and sent him to me. As I talked with the athlete, it became clear to me that he already had the skills necessary to shoot free throws, and changing his shooting style was unwarranted. However, I found out the player was unaware that increases in anxiety would interfere with his performance when he went to the free-throw line. His lack of awareness meant that he was unable to compensate for the increasing tension or to implement a procedure which would act to lower it. In effect the cues that were available to discriminate between levels of tension were not being used. My strategy then was to help him identify these cues.

I asked the player to tell me what he thought about and did from the time he was fouled until he actually attempted the free throw. He began to describe the process in general terms, "The ref tosses me the ball. I step to the line and I shoot." I told him that I wanted him to close his eyes, think through the entire sequence, and describe each detail. His comments were still too general, so I tried to elicit more precise responses from him. I asked him if he became angry after he was fouled. He told me that he did get angry sometimes, but once he stepped to the line he forgot about everything but the shot. I asked him to tell me how he stood at the line, what the position of his feet was, if he bent his knees, and so forth. Knowing that most basketball players bounce the ball before they shoot free throws, I asked him if he did this. He said that he did, but when I asked him how many times, he was unable to tell me. To facilitate his recall, I asked him to open his eyes, to stand up, and to shoot a free throw for me in the office. He did this after positioning his feet and bouncing the imaginary ball three times.

By standing up and going through his shot, he was forced to consciously direct his attention to what his body was doing. This conscious effort made it much easier for him to recall his feelings and to visualize what he was doing at the foul line. I asked him to sit down again and to reflect back on some of the free throws he had been missing. Suddenly he reported that on those occasions when he bounced the ball less than three times or more than four times he was likely to miss.

His discovery points out an important factor involved in the execution of a series of coordinated movements. Through practice, we all develop a natural rhythm and a sense of timing, and anything which interferes with our rhythm or timing throws us off stride and dramatically disrupts performance. I mentioned earlier that anxiety results in increases in muscle tension and thus produces an impairment in both timing and coordination, and this athlete's experience at the free-throw line is a good example of the process. As his anxiety increased, so did his desire to get on with the activity that would reduce his tension—shooting the ball. This means that he may have tried to speed up his normal response, and on such occasions he reduced the number of times he bounced the ball. Divers respond to anxiety by running for the end of the board instead of taking a normal approach. Bowlers and golfers find themselves pulling the ball or the club as they try to hurry through the activity. Even public speakers experience the same phenomenon. As their anxiety mounts, they find themselves breathing at the wrong time and racing through their talk. Often they speak so rapidly that the audience just hears a bunch of garbled words.

Bouncing the ball fewer than three times was a discriminative cue that the basketball player could use to tell himself he was becoming anxious. I should emphasize that he needed this cue to recognize his anxiety because initially he was not consciously aware of any feelings of increased muscle tension. On those occasions when he *had* been aware of feeling tense, he bounced the ball more than the usual number of times in an attempt to calm himself. He usually noticed that as he stepped to the line he was unable to get set. He did not feel "planted" on the line. It was as though his body were lighter than usual, and no matter how he stood, he didn't feel right. As a result he moved around at the line and kept bouncing the ball, trying to get the right feeling. As you have probably figured out by now, his attention was being directed inwardly to negative feelings and his focus on these feelings resulted in still more anxiety. The way to help him was to teach him to focus instead on those feelings and behaviors that would allow him to maintain his own natural rhythm and also to learn to control his level of arousal. It may sound complicated, but for him the cues to rehearse were fairly simple.

I told him that between the time the foul occurred and the moment he stepped into the free-throw circle, he was free to collect his thoughts and direct them in any way he wished. He could get angry, he could be thankful for a break in the action, he could plan ahead—whatever. The referee handing him the ball, however, was a discriminative cue that should remind him: (1) to step to the line, take a deep breath, and then exhale slowly; (2) as he felt himself settle down while exhaling, to dribble the ball three times; and (3) to bring his hand up in position to shoot. At this time he again exhaled and then executed the shot. If any part of the process was disturbed, he was instructed to step away from the free-throw line and start again. Through this process the athlete was able to regain his own natural rhythm and shoot the eyes out of the basket—at least from the foul line.

Rehearsal As a Means of Improving Technique

Here's a second example of the rehearsal process. To help my wife improve her bowling, I took her through relaxation procedures, then asked her to try to visualize and feel what it's like to bowl. She reported that she was able to feel the first step of her approach and to get the feeling of releasing the ball but that she was unable to examine what occurred in between. This response is not unusual. I asked her to stand up and go through an actual approach. Following this rehearsal, she was able mentally to develop the feelings and images that were associated with bowling. I asked her to mentally bowl a strike for me, telling her that it would be no problem since she had bowled them before. She tried to respond, but to my surprise she reported that she had left a couple of pins standing. She informed me that her imaginary ball had hit too far to the right of the headpin. I told her to move her position on the lane slightly to the left and to try again. This time she bowled an imaginary strike but reported that the new position made her feel a bit awkward. I told her that it was a natural response and not to worry about it. In contrast to the basketball player's focus on cues that indicated arousal, my wife needed to focus on cues that would help her become aware of the physical relationship of where and how she released the ball and the way it struck the pins. The difference between what the two individuals needed to focus on was due largely to their different levels of athletic development. My wife, I soon found out, still needed to learn the mechanics of bowling.

Rehearsal Problems

Using the two examples just presented, let me emphasize some of the important factors involved in the successful application of mental rehearsal procedures. First, it's important that rehearsal occur only when you are not actively engaged in the activity. Next, it's extremely important to rehearse a large enough segment of the behavior so that your natural rhythm is maintained. Only then can you find where your mistakes actually begin. Many athletes have come to me after they have already attempted to use some kind of rehearsal procedure to detect and correct errors.

When they fail, it's often because they did not move far enough back into the behavioral chain. For example, a golfer noticed that his club head was coming down too quickly, resulting in his turning his hips out at the wrong time. To compensate for this, he rehearsed slowing down the top part of his downswing. This failed to help because it broke up his rhythm and gave him a choppy swing. In fact his swing began just as he addressed the ball, and his rehearsal process should have begun at this point. He needed to slow down the entire backswing as well as the top of his downswing.

Another reason that some athletes are unable to use a rehearsal process effectively is that, not at all surprisingly, they focus on the wrong cues for particular situations. For example, if you have already developed a high degree of skill, one use of rehearsal procedures is for you to identify and learn to focus in game situations only on those particular cues that would maximize your ability to respond in a natural, reflexive way. Mentally the basketball player directs his attention toward taking a deep breath, bouncing the ball three times, or whatever has helped him shoot fouls in the past. One vital aspect of the rehearsal processes is to make the athlete aware of these critical cues in the game itself. In brief he learns through rehearsal what he should be doing and he learns to maintain this focus of attention through mental practice.

A second very valuable use of rehearsal procedures is to analyze the technical aspects of performance. On these occasions the goal is to become aware of the relationships between bodily feelings and the actual performance. For example, you may focus attention on learning to recognize feelings of muscle tension in your fingers, wrist, forearm, and shoulder as you execute a jump shot. You learn to become sensitive to the differences between these feelings when you score two points as opposed to when you miss.

During rehearsal practice you take the time to think about each physical element of the shot and how it feels. In actual competition, however, you cannot think in this fashion because to do so would destroy concentration on the game and your rhythm. Ideally, through reflecting back on past performance and through rehearsal off the court, you learn what the good shot feels like. Then, like the automatic memory of the players' positions on a baseball diamond, when something goes wrong during competition, a particular feeling tells you what you did incorrectly. In this way, during the game you do not have to attend consciously to all the things you're doing in order to find out what is going wrong—you just *know*. Naturally the development of this ability greatly simplifies the demands of a competitive situation.

The major problem associated with the effective use of rehearsal procedures is the determination of what the discriminative cues should be for a particular athlete in a particular situation. Just as athletes actually practice bad techniques, so individuals engaging in rehearsal concentrate on the wrong cues and as with most situations, there are usually more wrong answers than right answers available. In most instances inappropriate rehearsal procedures simply have no effect on the individual's performance, but it *is* possible to rehearse in ways which actually interfere. In the next few paragraphs, therefore, I would like to provide you with a strategy for deciding what discriminative cues you as an individual should focus on.

The Selection of Discriminative Cues

Begin by picking a specific activity you want to work on. This activity should have a distinct start and finish and should be fairly short in terms of the length of time required to complete it. Examples of things you might choose to focus on include: using a particular type of club or executing a particular shot in golf, a specific tennis stroke, a turn in swimming, a certain dive or movement in gymnastics, or a single play in football. Again, the important points are that the activity have an identifiable start and finish and that it require only a few seconds to actually complete.

Once you have selected a problem, the discriminative cues need to be identified. You must decide whether the focus and rehearsal are to be aimed at keeping anxiety to a minimum and maintaining a rhythm or whether they are intended to improve or sharpen a particular skill. Look at the behavior you have chosen to work on and then ask yourself if your goal is to improve the consistency of performance. If you decide that you want to play consistently at a level that you have occasionally reached in the past, then your focus should be on learning to discriminate changes in tension levels which affect your performance. On the other hand, if your goal is to exceed your optimal performance in the past, the focus may need to be on developing new techniques and changing old responses. Whatever the focus, the process for identifying the discriminative cues is very similar.

There are several methods to select the appropriate cues to focus on. The first and most obvious is to ask someone experienced and aware of the physical and psychological demands of the particular skill you hope to develop to study your game films or actual performance. Once again, the pulling together of the collective knowledge of a coach and a psychologist is ideal. Books are another source of expert opinion. However, once you have an idea of the way your body should feel and move theoretically, you need to be able to describe how it actually does feel and move.

Begin this by actually practicing the activity a number of

times. First pay attention to the feelings in specific parts of your body at specific points in the activity. Then just practice a few more times with a smooth, natural flow, completing the entire activity and not calling your attention to *any* particular part or movement. Following this practice, you ought to be able to sit down and recall the various related feelings in your body as you went through the entire activity. The steps that proceed from this awareness will be most useful to you in deciding what you need to focus on. The trick is to become aware of when you are performing either correctly or incorrectly—that is, to be able to discriminate between the two. Happily there are several strategies which you can use to discover the cues that lead to this discrimination.

With respect to the development of a new technique, you must mentally produce a composite picture of how the behavior looks and feels when it is performed correctly. Again, this can be accomplished by getting the help of experts to point out things like the ideal hand position, how your body weight should be distributed, and so forth. You can also watch films and analyze still photographs and actually model the positions in which you see other athletes. Once you know the correct techniques, then slowly go through the activity in your mind the same way *you had been doing it in the past*. Then carefully compare your own way of performing with the ideal way. In reality there may be more than one ideal technique, but you probably would have chosen the technique closest to your own, since you would feel most comfortable with it. Now comes the important step. The discrepancies you notice are *your* discriminative cues. Use them to correct past errors as you mentally rehearse the correct technique.

When you move into actual practice, take only the first discriminative cue in the activity and work with it until you are performing that aspect of the endeavor correctly. This might mean, for instance, eliminating your dribble before taking your jump shot (this presupposes that you know your spot on the court) because the time spent dribbling allows the defender to close in on you. Then move through the entire activity one cue at a time, working on each area of imperfection until the right moves come naturally—that is, you don't have to think them through anymore. Your body in effect is thinking for itself. All that rehearsal has now produced a hit!

As you progress, keep a practiced eye open for three possibilities. First, you may begin to discover additional discriminative cues as you go along. Second, you may find that correction of one part of your performance will temporarily disrupt other aspects which initially were no problem. Don't sweat it—just work easily and slowly, and performance will quickly return to normal. Finally, you will probably find that as earlier errors are corrected, some of the problems that occurred later in the activity automatically disappear. For example, if you notice that in bowling you are both rushing the foul line and releasing the ball too high, you may find that slowing your approach also causes you to bend over more. Thus both problems are corrected with a single change in technique.

Exaggerate the Mistakes

One additional note here may prove helpful. If you find that you're having difficulty identifying cues that tell you what your body feels like when you're performing correctly, as opposed to what it feels like when you're performing incorrectly, the following strategy may be helpful. I had a diver who couldn't tell if her legs were bent and her toes pointed down. She simply was unable to feel the difference. To work around this, I had her first exaggerate and attend to an incorrect response. "Just jump, but bend your knees and make your feet as flat as you can. Look at your toes and curl them up." After going through this awkward procedure a few times, I had her look at her legs and concentrate on the physical feelings experienced when she jumped with her legs together and toes pointed—the correct stance. This exaggeration of a mistake was useful in finally making her aware of what her body was doing. The contrast in the two feelings provided the discriminative cues and she was then able to mentally rehearse and feel her body in the correct stance.

The procedures for identifying the discriminative cues needed to learn to maintain a consistent level of performance are not too dissimilar from those presented above. Fortunately, because the athlete already has the skills required, some additional techniques are possible.

As with learning some new procedure, the best way to discover the discriminative cues needed to increase awareness and control over tension is to contrast two different levels of *your own* performance and then focus on their differences. To do this, sit down and mentally take yourself through some past performances. You should fairly quickly be able to recall kinesthetic cues that are associated with both good and bad performance. Again, remember to keep the rehearsal limited to a single task, such as the execution of a backhand in tennis. If you find you are having trouble doing this on the mental level, pay particular attention to bodily feelings the next time you practice. This will certainly make it easier for you to recall them later. Mentally you might suggest to yourself that you examine both a well-executed and poorly executed backhand in the following way.

It's important that during any rehearsal process you attempt to maintain a passive attitude. That's why the relaxation procedures are part of it. The idea is to be able to observe, in a passive, objective way, your own performance and feelings. You play the role of both observer (coach) and participant (athlete). The coach calls attention to the important aspects of performance; the athlete passively listens, executes the movements, and observes his own feelings. To experience this, try to assume both the coach's and the athlete's roles in the next example.

Rehearsal of a Backhand

Closing your eyes, decide first to concentrate on the way you *should* hit the shot. Relax and watch yourself stroke the ball and then slow it up and rerun it a step at a time, breaking it up into short but important segments which have been chosen with a tennis coach. As an example, you might begin by noticing your position on the court just as your opponent begins to hit the ball to you. Are you back deep on the court? Are you leaning in any direction? Are you facing the net? What position are your arms and legs in? As you move and get set to hit the ball, and as you actually start your backswing, notice the following: How are you holding the racquet? Where are your toes pointed? How far apart are your feet? What is the position of your legs, and how are they supporting the weight of your body—on the front leg, the back leg, both legs? Where is the strain on the muscles? Are your knees bent? How is your body now positioned relative to the net? Where are you looking? How do the muscles in your shoulder, upper arm, forearm, and wrist feel? How far back do you bring the racquet?

Now, as you swing the racquet forward, notice the changes which occur. How are you holding the racquet? Are you inhaling or holding your breath? Where is the thumb on your racquet hand? How does your body weight shift as you swing through the ball? How does this change if you want to alter the placement of your shot? What is the position of your body relative to the net? Where are you looking? What is the position of the racquet head as it strikes the ball? At this exact point in time, where are you looking? What do the muscles in your wrist, arm, and shoulder feel like? Finally, as you follow through, note the changes once again in body position. How far do you follow through? Where is the racquet head pointing? When do you begin to turn to face the net?

To get a strong sense of the rehearsal process, you might put the above questions on tape or simply have someone read them to you slowly, with about a three- to five-second pause between each question. Go through them twice: the first time recall your hitting the ball correctly and the second time recall a poor return.

Once again, the discriminative cues for you are those feelings that indicate a discrepancy between the two shots. Your legs may feel awkward or you may not shift your grip properly or you may not get positioned in time. Once you have identified the differences, then several times rapidly rehearse correcting the discrepancy. For example, think several times of shifting your forehand grip to a backhand grip. *Of course it is important, if you already know how to hit the ball correctly and are working on consistency, to keep your rehearsal out of the actual competitive situation.* You are trying to reach the point where you do not think about the shot during actual competition, you simply execute it. And then, *because you are now so aware of your body and how it* should *feel,* any discrepancy will be easily noticed. *After the point is over,* however, you may have the time to rehearse correcting your mistake, but even then the rehearsal process should only be used if you are able to engage in it objectively. If you find yourself swearing at yourself while you are mentally making the correction, you may well be increasing tension rather than reducing it. This anger could easily be carried over into the next exchange and would act to interfere with concentration and performance.

Each of us reacts differently to our mistakes. You may be able to get angry momentarily and then completely forget about it as soon as you get into position for the next shot. In any case, you must look to your own performance to discover which type of individual you are. *If you have difficulty maintaining control, then you definitely should learn to wait until the game is over to rehearse your mistakes.* Ideally you would rehearse and correct as you go along, but the nature of competition generally makes this highly unlikely.

Error Consistency As an Indication of Arousal

A final and very interesting rehearsal process for you to experiment with is determining whether or not you can detect any pattern to the type of mistakes that you make in a particular competitive situation. Quite apart from correcting each mistake as it occurs, it would be most valuable to be able to identify why the mistakes occur in the first place. This knowledge can be gained through identifying the similarities in the mistakes you make. When relationships between errors appear to exist, they can provide the information that tells you what you're doing wrong and hopefully what you can do to avoid these mistakes in the future.

As an example, I worked with an International Skeet Shooter who was extremely surprised when an analysis revealed a high proportion of misses on a relatively simple target. His error pattern told us that concentration (as a function of overconfidence) was being disturbed at this point. Just the new awareness of this trouble spot was enough to correct the concentration loss.

Do remember, though, that some apparent errors are not errors at all. There is no apparent reason for them, they just happen—the ball may take a bad bounce or the wind may shift. However, if you are making the same type of error in several different situations or making a string of errors in one particular situation, the problem is real and usually has to do with arousal and the resultant changes in muscle tension and your ability to concentrate. Moreover, the tension may or may not be limited to a particular muscle group.

As an example of such a constellation of tension, let me reintroduce you to the bowler mentioned earlier in this chapter who improved his game average by twenty pins. This athlete noticed that when he was performing poorly, the following series of discrepancies from his better performances occurred: (1) he noted tension in his chest and back muscles as he stood at the head of the lane; (2) he found himself looking back and forth from his ball to his mark more times than usual; (3) he found that he pulled the ball through (because he was rushing to the line too quickly); (4) he noticed he did not bend over as far when he attempted to release the ball; (5) finally, he found that he was pulling his arm across in front of his body as he released the ball. All of these cues, taken both collectively and individually, can be explained in terms of increased muscle tension in his neck, arms, and shoulders. Rather than attempting to rehearse and correct each one of these individual mistakes, it was advisable for him first to practice relaxation procedures and then to rehearse bowling correctly.

When the cause is clearly anxiety, the focus should be on tension reduction or on stimuli which help the individual avoid focusing on his failures, whatever these may be. Consistency has to happen before improvement can occur. Thus under these conditions the imagery and rehearsal procedures you use should focus on pleasant, positive thoughts and feelings rather than on errors. Success has to be built from past successes in this case.

Mental rehearsal procedures, when they are effective, work because they teach you to direct attention to those cues which are most important for your performance. This means, among other things, that you learn to control your level of arousal because you are able to direct attention either toward or away from anxiety-inducing stimuli. In addition you learn to deal with more complex situations, not because you are now able to think any faster, but because you are able to be more selective about what you attend to.

The Peak Experience

In that regard you may remember that in Chapter 1, I talked about those rare occasions when an athlete is having such a super day that things seem to float, to occur almost in slow motion. I gave my own example of diving, but it's the same in other sports. Movements of opponents seem slowed so that it becomes easy to hit the fast ball or dodge a tackler. You are able to anticipate others' moves well in advance. These changes in your time sense can be explained on the basis of changes in your heightened attentional processes.

To reverse things, think of your eyes as a motion picture camera and imagine that you are standing at home plate, getting ready to hit a baseball. Under normal circumstances you watch the ball closely, but every so often your attention to the ball is distracted by a thought or an image or by something going on around you. These distractions, brief though they may be, cut frames out of the motion picture that your eyes are filming. The more anxious you are, the more distractions that occur and the more the film is spliced. In effect, as anxiety increases, you are spending less and less time watching the pitcher's windup and delivery. As you get really anxious, you begin to feel as though things are happening too quickly. The film is speeded up and your world suddenly resembles a 1920 Charlie Chaplin movie.

Even under normal circumstances, however, there is a certain amount of editing going on and the film is almost always speeded up more than it ought to be under ideal circumstances. Thus as you experience fewer distractions than normal, the experience is one of slow motion. On those days that you feel as if you are hanging in the air, looping in long jump shots, you spend more time than usual attending to relevant cues. What has transpired is that you are totally immersed in your play and you have lost all awareness of yourself. You flow with the activity and it is only later, when you have returned to your normal, critical self, that you realize how totally involved you have been.

To summarize, then, through the use of mental rehearsal processes you can begin to train yourself to recognize what the important cues are in competitive situations. Through learning what you should be attending to and through practicing passive concentration, you also become more capable of recognizing when you are becoming distracted and are able to break away from the distractions more quickly. This combination of attentional changes results in greater involvement in the activity and possibly in an increase in peak experiences. Finally, by becoming aware of what you should be experiencing in an athletic situation you learn to recognize mistakes which would have passed unnoticed before and which now can be avoided.

Chapter 10. **Biofeedback**

In the previous chapters a great deal of emphasis has been placed on pointing out how anxiety and tension act to interfere with both mental and physical performance. In addition it was pointed out that the ability to detect tension increases is critical if you hope to maintain control over your arousal level and thus your performance. Too often we do not become aware of increasing arousal until it is too late and we are already out of control, and so this awareness is vital.

However, it is not enough just to know what is going on—you must also be able to do something about it. Biofeedback promises to provide each of us with a very direct way of learning what our bodies are doing and of learning how to control them.

Before getting into biofeedback, I would like to give the very briefest of reviews to other methods for gaining control over mental processes. Through procedures like hypnosis, meditation, and various forms of autogenic training you *can* learn to control your attentional processes. Then almost as a side effect you will discover that your physical feelings and attentional processes are closely related. Control over attention leads to control over physiology. In some ways biofeedback almost seems like the reverse of this process. As you will be shown in this chapter, by learning to control physiological responses through biofeedback, you may suddenly realize that you have also learned to direct and control attention.

Biofeedback History

Studies of human and animal learning have taught us that one of the most effective and rapid ways for learning to take place is for the organism to have immediate feedback about its performance. What seems critical in the learning process, however, is a knowledge of what effect a planned adjustment or a spontaneous change in attitude will have on bodily functions. For many of the activities we engage in, the feedback is immediately available in the form of visual, auditory, and kinesthetic cues. When you are learning to shoot baskets, for example, you notice that certain bodily feelings are associated with the shot and you can see and hear how successful you are. If you miss the shot because you didn't shoot hard enough, you know that you need to increase your strength. In this example all the information you need in order to learn to shoot baskets is immediately available to you and fairly easy to recognize.

Unfortunately the ability to learn to control anxiety and internal bodily processes is *not* so easy. Without knowing the changes occurring within your body, you cannot be aware of the effect of these changes on your performance. Under such conditions, trying to learn to control a biological process such as muscle tension, heart rate, blood pressure, etc., would be like trying to shoot baskets with numb muscles, while wearing ear plugs, and in complete darkness. Under these conditions you would be amazingly lucky to hit the backboard, much less the basket.

Recognizing the importance of immediate feedback to learning, Dr. Neale Miller, a scientist at Rockefeller University in New York City, began experimenting on animals in the late 1950s to find out if they could learn to control bodily processes when provided with a reward for making the changes the experimenter desired. It is from this work that the term biofeedback developed. All the term implies is that feedback or information about the subject's ongoing biological processes is available for use in providing indications of changes going on within the body. What Dr. Miller did was to devise ways of recording changes in either heart rate or blood pressure in rats; then he used these results to either reward or punish the animal for the changes which occurred. For example, if Dr. Miller wanted the animal to learn to increase blood pressure, he watched an instrument which provided constant readings of the rat's blood pressure. Then, when a slight increase occurred in the blood pressure, Dr. Miller rewarded the animal. Gradually, after many rewards, the rat learned to increase his blood pressure. Then, when a slight increase occurred in the blood it was discovered that if animals were motivated either to avoid punishment or to get some pleasurable sensation, they could be taught to control many processes which in the past were assumed out of the organisms' conscious control.[1]

The studies by Miller were exciting because they suggested that human beings might one day learn to gain control over processes like blood pressure and in so doing gain some control over illnesses associated with or resulting from hypertension. The major problem in applying Miller's methodology to human research had to do with finding new ways of providing feedback to the individual. For example, to provide constant monitoring and feedback about a rat's blood pressure, it was necessary to insert a catheter into the rat's abdominal aorta (the main trunk of the arterial system carrying blood away from the heart). There are few human subjects willing to undergo such a process. The traditional method of measuring blood pressure by using an inflatable cuff is not suitable because monitorings cannot be continuous and feedback cannot be presented quickly enough. In addition, experimental procedures and proper controls had not been worked out to the point of justifying such experimentation on humans.

Alpha Feedback

It wasn't until the late 1960s that the public began to find out about biofeedback. This occurred with the appearance of reports on some work by Dr. Joseph Kamiya conducted at the Langley Porter Neuropsychiatric Institute in San Francisco.[2] Kamiya, taking off from the work of Miller and others, wanted to see if human beings could learn to tell what brain wave state they were experiencing at a particular time. He knew from the research literature that it was possible, through the use of an electroencephalograph or EEG, to measure and record the electrical activity of the brain and to identify several different brain wave states. Kamiya was interested in seeing if subjects could learn by monitoring their own feelings to tell when they were in two of these states, alpha and beta.

Theoretically, learning to make such a discrimination should not be too difficult. Ever since the 1930s, researchers have believed that the alpha state (synchronized brain waves between a frequency of eight and thirteen cycles per second) is associated with being relaxed and not focusing attention. Beta waves (fast, desynchronized, low-amplitude waves between a frequency of fifteen and forty cycles per second) on the other hand are assumed to be associated with focused attention and concentration. Figure 10.1 presents an example of these two types of brain waves.

Dr. Kamiya monitored his subjects' brain waves and at various points rang a bell and asked them to guess whether they had an A or B type of activity. He discovered that within a few hours subjects could learn to discriminate between the two states. Following this discrimination training he attempted to see if the subjects, having learned to recognize their brain-wave states, could produce alpha waves on demand. He found that they could.

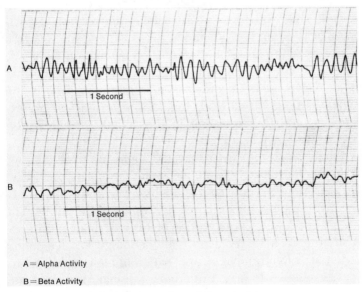

A = Alpha Activity

B = Beta Activity

Figure 10.1   Brain Wave Activity

Kamiya then set up a feedback system in which the subjects were continuously informed whether they were in an alpha or beta state. This was accomplished by constructing electronic devices designed to detect the presence of alpha. The subjects were connected to the equipment, and when alpha was recognized a signal was given the subjects in the form of a light and/or a tone. If the signal was on, the individuals knew that they were in alpha, and if it was off, they knew they were not. The subjects were then asked to try to learn to keep the tone on. Over a few hours individuals began to learn what bodily feelings and thought processes were associated with the tone, and they demonstrated that they could maintain it.

Apart from learning to control brain waves, subjects began reporting and describing what they felt when they were in the alpha state. This was a real breakthrough—individuals spontaneously began to describe their experience in alpha as being similar to a meditative state, reporting that they felt relaxed and at peace. They experienced a "oneness with nature" and described having a noncritical, passive attention—the type of attentional process that has been discussed in several previous chapters. This is the type of attention that leads to a loss of personal awareness and a complete immersion in the activity in which you happen to be engaged.

Since the studies by Miller and Kamiya a large number of individuals have become interested in biofeedback. The result is that several companies are currently marketing feedback equipment for home use. Some of the equipment is very good, but a large portion of it is just about worthless. Also, the rush to try a new methodology has led many individuals to attempt the application of biofeedback training procedures to a vast number of human problems and conditions. The overwhelming majority of these applications are uncontrolled, and the results obtained are highly suspect. In addition individuals with no apparent knowledge of the relationship between feedback and learning theory, nor with any understanding of the principles of reinforcement, are applying these techniques in haphazard ways.

The result is that it is difficult for the average reader to separate fiction and fantasy from fact. Companies make exaggerated claims, journalists sensationalize, and quacks fleece the public. Nevertheless, through a responsible look at what is happening, I believe it *is* possible to gain some realistic hold on the potential applications of biofeedback to athletics, although to date little work has actually been done in this area.

After all, what *isn't* fantasy is that biofeedback procedures have been used to treat a vast array of medical and psychological problems. Selected readings on the clinical applications of biofeedback are provided at the end of this book for those who are interested.[3] Despite the growing literature those clinical applications that have the most direct transfer to athletics are those which involve training subjects to control muscle tension levels.

Procedures for Providing Feedback

A considerable amount of research has been conducted which indicates quite clearly that with feedback from various muscle groups—attained through the use of an EMG (electromyograph)—subjects can learn to alter tension levels. What's involved is measuring the electrical activity of particular muscle groups—the more tension in the muscles, the more electrical activity. This energy is amplified and used to operate a light or tone generator, and the subject, through listening to changes in the tone, becomes aware of changes in muscle tension. For example, you might be interested in becoming aware of—and controlling—the muscle tension in your shoulders since control over these particular muscles are important to a variety of sports, including tennis, golf, gymnastics, and diving.

To provide training, electrodes (discs used to pick up the electrical activity of the muscles) are attached to the muscles running from your neck to your shoulder. Don't worry about this procedure—all it involves, physically, is using some paste to temporarily attach a small piece of metal to the surface of your skin. It's painless and much like applying a Band-Aid. The electrode picks up the current from the relevant muscles (the current may be as small as one millionth of a volt) and transmits it to an amplifier, which in turn magnifies the energy until it is of sufficient intensity to operate a feedback device. Usually the equipment is designed so that as you tense your muscles, a feedback tone increases in pitch, and as you relax, it decreases. Your task then, when hooked up, is to listen to the tone and to learn what you can do to increase or decrease the pitch.[4]

Through research on feedback, we know that in a fairly short period of time individuals do learn to control various muscle groups. Some of the muscles which have been monitored and controlled include jaw, neck, shoulder, chest, forehead, and those of the arm. And actual medical application of this type of training has found it useful for treatment of any illness that is caused by, or aggravated by, excessive muscle tension—for instance, headaches, muscular soreness, neck injury, and stuttering. Moreover, the ability to increase tension in particular muscles has been taught to subjects in order to help them compensate for a deficiency. Feedback of facial muscle tension, for example, has been used to teach blind individuals to develop facial expressions that are appropriate for their feelings (for example, to smile when they are happy).

Although, as I mentioned earlier, little direct work has been conducted with athletes, it is certainly possible to take some of these clinical applications and generalize them to athletic situations.

Biofeedback and Pain

One of the major theories about the experience of pain has to do with small subclinical muscle spasms which are not directly observable. Theoretically, pain results through these spasms, which cause a reaction in pain receptor cells in the afflicted area.[5] More obvious than these subclinical manifestations is the obvious increase in pain and in the severity of an injury when you can actually feel excess muscle tension pull on ligaments and tissues. The application of biofeedback of muscle tension in or around these injured areas could be used by an athlete to learn to reduce tension and thus reduce pain and muscle soreness. Such an application has already been used clinically in the treatment of patients with neck injuries, and we have used it successfully as a part of the treatment of "overuse" syndromes such as tendonitis (tennis elbow) when muscles are involved as well as tendons.

Discriminating Between Relevant and Irrelevant Muscle Tension

An obvious application of muscle tension feedback involves training an athlete to be aware of changes in muscle tension in those muscles that are critical for his particular event or sport. As an example, I have been working with a swimmer in an attempt to get her to minimize and maximize muscle tension during the breast stroke. First I provide feedback from a relevant muscle group, such as neck, shoulders, and forehead. Next I have her go through a relaxation procedure, and then I have her mentally rehearse a race. When she engages in the rehearsal, she attempts to lower muscle tension as she glides and increase it as she strokes. Slowly she learns to develop a rhythm and her attention becomes directed to that. Thus far the procedures have resulted in a large decrease in her anxiety just prior to and during competition. In addition her times are improving with each meet.

The procedure that I have just described is actually a combination of several treatment approaches. Perhaps some of the best uses of biofeedback will ultimately involve its being used as an adjunct to various other approaches. In fact there is one such combination which already appears very promising. This involves the use of biofeedback of muscle tension in conjunction with a treatment approach called systematic desensitization.

Systematic Desensitization

Systematic desensitization is a term applied to a particular type of psychotherapy. Theoretically it works because it is impossible for a person to feel both anxious and relaxed at the same time, but in practice the therapeutic process is little more than the combination of a relaxation procedure and mental rehearsal. The treatment is designed to help the patient deal effectively with a certain fear. In athletics, for example, it might be used to help an end overcome his fear of bodily contact when he is trying to catch the football or it might be used to aid a batter who has been hit by a pitched ball to overcome his fear of that happening again. Whatever the fear, once it is identified, you begin to develop a fear hierarchy.

The Fear Hierarchy

The fear hierarchy involves nothing more than defining and ranking eight to ten situations that cause progressive increases in the amount of fear they elicit. Let's say you selected a fear that involves being hit in the head by a pitched ball. The lowest item on your hierarchy, the point where you first begin to experience anxiety, might involve sitting in the dugout just before you are due to come to bat. The most fearful situation for you, the highest point on the hierarchy, might involve standing in the batter's box and observing a pitch that is coming at you high and inside. Table 10.1 presents a hypothetical fear hierarchy.

Once a hierarchy is developed, you are taught to employ a relaxation procedure that builds up your ability to relax. Then, after a week or two of working on these procedures, desensitization treatment begins. To begin the treatment, the psychologist asks you to relax—using whatever proce-

Table 10.1   Hitter's Fear Hierarchy

1. Sitting in the dugout just before going to bat
2. Standing in the batting circle, warming up
3. Walking to the plate
4. Walking to the plate against a particular pitcher
5. Seeing the hitter in front of me step back to avoid being hit
6. Standing in the batter's box
7. Seeing the hitter in front of me hit by a pitch
8. Watching a pitch that is coming high and inside

dure works for you—and then asks you to indicate on a scale ranging from zero to ten how relaxed you are. On this scale, zero means that you are not relaxed at all and ten means you are as relaxed as possible. To find out how relaxed you are, the psychologist calls off numbers starting with zero. Once he reaches your level of relaxation, you indicate it by raising the index finger on your right hand. Let's assume that you reach a level of seven. Next he asks you to begin visualizing the first item on the fear hierarchy. For instance, he asks you to imagine that you are sitting in the dugout just before going to bat. After you have imagined this scene, the psychologist again calls off the numbers of the relaxation scale. As he calls out five, you raise your finger, indicating that the visual imagery has caused you to become slightly more aroused. More instructions are given to relax (you may give them to yourself), and then the same item is visualized again. As soon as you are able to maintain your relaxed feelings and still visualize sitting in the dugout, you move to visualizing the second item on the hierarchy. Slowly, over eight to sixteen sessions, you work your way to the point of being able to imagine yourself watching a pitch that is coming high and inside without becoming anxious.

Through the systematic desensitization procedures just described, psychologists have been effective in dramatically reducing or eliminating between seventy and ninety per cent of the fears that individuals wish to deal with. A vast majority of the people treated in this fashion reach the point of behaviorally conquering their fear—that is, they engage in activities they would not have attempted prior to treatment. Moreover, with the introduction of biofeedback, systematic desensitization as a treatment promises to become even more efficient. In fact, in our laboratory we have been working out a set of self-treatment procedures for individuals who want to become more relaxed in performance situations. In effect the athletes treat themselves with a minimum of professional supervision.

Biofeedback and Systematic Desensitization

Biofeedback is used as an adjunct to systematic desensitization by employing the feedback of muscle tension as a much more sensitive indicator of tension changes than the individual's own subjective report. Remember the problem I discussed earlier—that very often athletes are unaware of tension increases until it is too late. Well, the constant recording of muscle tension during treatment, via biofeedback equipment, allows both the psychologist and the athlete to become aware of tension changes sooner. The psychologist no longer has to ask the athlete to rate anxiety subjectively. If he sees that anxiety is increasing as visualization occurs, he can immediately stop the visualization process and get the subject to relax again.

As you can see, the addition of biofeedback to an already successful procedure provides a more sensitive indicator of changes in anxiety and at the same time makes the subject more sensitive and aware of his arousal. This last point can be very important for you when you are first learning to relax.

Biofeedback and Autogenic Training

One of the biggest problems individuals encounter when they attempt to learn autogenic training or some other form of progressive relaxation is that they don't know if they are practicing in the proper way. Early in their training they aren't aware of slight changes in their arousal level and thus don't know whether or not they are relaxing. Fortunately biofeedback of muscle tension can now be used to provide an early indication of whether relaxation is developing or not. Through feedback the individual gets immediate reinforcement for relaxing, and there is no question about whether what is supposed to be happening is in fact happening.

When biofeedback procedures are used to augment some progressive relaxation exercise, they are usually employed only once or twice a week. Thus you would come in for a biofeedback session that involves recording of muscle tension while you are relaxing. Following this, you are instructed to go home and practice the relaxation procedures twice a day for the remainder of the week. This process is then repeated until you have successfully mastered the procedures.

Feedback of EEG Activity

Thus far I have been talking about using feedback of muscle tension to help you improve performance. Another type of feedback that may be promising involves the feedback of the electrical activity from your brain.

Clinically, feedback of brain wave activity has been used to teach people to relax. This has been accomplished by having them attempt to maintain an alpha wave state. The alpha state, as mentioned earlier, is associated with being relaxed and not focusing attention in a problem-solving way. In addition EEG feedback has been used with some success to treat patients with insomnia. The application of this type of feedback to athletics is considerably more speculative than EMG feedback, yet some possibilities are apparent.

It does seem likely that EEG feedback of both alpha and theta waves[6] can be helpful in teaching some athletes to go to sleep the night before a big game. In addition it has been suggested that in order to maintain a high degree of alpha activity, many individuals find themselves developing a passive concentration—the type of attentional focus that is so important to meditation and progressive relaxation. For this reason alpha feedback might be useful both as a procedure for teaching individuals to relax and as a method for teaching them how to avoid becoming distracted by irrelevant stimuli. It's not inconceivable that alpha might provide an indirect, yet rapid way of teaching some individuals to develop the passive concentration that is necessary to keep from "choking" in tense competitive situations. *Because alpha is not as abundant, however, when a person is focusing on or tracking visual objects, it's very unlikely that an athlete would be in alpha during competition.*

Let the Buyer Beware

My comments about alpha feedback have been very cautious because many individuals are making promises for this type of procedure that are patently ridiculous. The development and use of biofeedback procedures are still in their infancy, and a great many questions remain to be answered about the ultimate effectiveness of these procedures. Despite this, far-out claims about increasing extrasensory perception, gaining control over disease processes, increasing intelligence, becoming creative, and increasing physical strength are being made. These claims simply cannot be substantiated, and in many cases are simply out-and-out lies.

However, I firmly believe that the biofeedback of muscle tension and possibly EEG activity has some very promising applications to athletics. Biofeedback, particularly of muscle tension, may be useful in the treatment of injuries—that is, as a method of helping to reduce pain and to assist the athlete in avoiding aggravation of injured tissue. It can also be used to assist the individual in learning to become aware of what specific muscle groups are doing (and should be doing) during particular situations. Finally, it is quite helpful in teaching a subject to relax—a procedure of considerable use to the athlete.

As a psychological treatment procedure, biofeedback appears to be effective for several reasons. First, the use of complicated electronics equipment and the feedback of minute electrical signals are impressive in and of themselves. This technological display is often enough to develop the faith and confidence athletes need to motivate them to stick with the process long enough for it to work. Thus for those athletes who are turned off by hypnosis or meditation (because of philosophical or ideological differences), biofeedback may be an alternative. As with the other treatment procedures mentioned, one of the major effects of biofeedback training is to teach individuals to gain control over their attentional processes. Subjects learn to relax by developing a passive-reflective attentional focus, and in many ways the feedback signal acts like the hypnotist's voice or the meditator's mantra, drawing attention away from anxiety-inducing thoughts into neutral areas.

On the other hand, the problems associated with the use of biofeedback are numerous. First of all, the equipment is expensive. Individuals who wish to buy reliable equipment for EMG feedback should be prepared to pay at least $500.[7] The price for reliable EEG feedback equipment is generally in the same area. A second problem is that some knowledge of learning theory (how, when, and what kind of feedback to provide) as well as a knowledge of biology and electrophysiology are required. Either the individual has to take several training courses or else he hires an expert—in either case, adding to his expense. A third problem is more specific to EEG feedback. Surprisingly enough, there are a great many people who do not have enough alpha wave activity to provide them with feedback. If they cannot develop alpha in the first place, they obviously cannot learn to maintain it.[8]

Chapter Eleven. **A Locker Room Wrapup**

Quite often I finish a talk on the psychology of athletics and delude myself by thinking that I have so thoroughly covered the subject that the audience could not possibly have any questions. What I invariably find, however, is that I have raised more questions than I have answered. I have had the opportunity to present much of the material covered in this book to a variety of audiences and they have never failed to come up with many interesting, important questions. Anticipating that some of their questions may also be on your mind, I think it only fitting that I end this book by discussing them.

Are you saying that hypnosis, biofeedback, autogenic training, and meditation are really the same thing?

Obviously these procedures differ from each other in many ways. They differ with respect to the number of outside people involved in working with you and with regard to the type of professional person directing or controlling the experience. Also they obviously differ in terms of the theory and philosophy behind their use. In spite of these differences, however, I believe that these procedures can be used to achieve the same ends. In addition I believe that when they are used successfully to teach an individual to lower arousal and to avoid "choking," it is because they have all made use of the same critical element.

Hypnosis, autogenic training, meditation, and biofeedback can be used to teach individuals to develop a passive type of concentration. Passive concentration is the type of attention that allows you to mirror (reflect) what is going on around you. You need to maintain this type of attention in order to avoid "choking," and it's the type of attention necessary to become completely immersed in an experience. Under these conditions there is a loss of identity in the sense that you are no longer emotionally reacting to and criticizing what is happening to you. Instead you are simply experiencing it.

It is this passive, nonevaluative attitude that allows the body to relax and rest, and this accounts for the physiological changes associated with these procedures. In each instance the ability to avoid becoming trapped in arousing thoughts develops through being taught to direct attention to some pleasant or neutral stimulus and in becoming more immune to distractions when they do occur. The particular stimulus you attend to varies from procedure to procedure. With meditation it is a mantra; with autogenics it is a standard formula; with biofeedback it is a light or tone; and with hypnosis it is the hypnotist's voice and suggestions.

Can't hypnosis be used to increase your strength?

Hypnosis, as I emphasized earlier, is not a mystical or supernatural state. Through relaxation and more focused concentration, you may sometimes function closer to your optimal level. At no time, however, do you perform at a level beyond your capabilities.

I have heard that meditation and the idea of passive concentration will ultimately lead to the athlete's losing his motivation to compete. Is this true?

No, nothing could be farther from the truth! In fairness to those spreading this myth, however, it develops quite naturally out of a misunderstanding of what passive concentration is and how it is used.

Athletes by nature are often extremely competitive. They have it drummed into their heads—by themselves and by others—that they must win, that they must be *the best*. Persons with this win-at-all-cost attitude find it absurd that under competitive conditions they must not care about a mistake or about being behind. The immediate response is that if you don't care, you won't improve and you won't be a winner. Caring and worrying certainly are important and they do serve to motivate you, but doing this during a contest only increases tension and distracts you from the task at hand. The trick is for you to learn to care and worry during practice or during breaks in the action, but to shut that out during the game. Actually, because of the energy saved and the free feelings associated with becoming completely involved in the contest, athletes usually find themselves *more* motivated to practice after meditating.

You talked about people having attentional styles. Aren't there some people whose attentional processes just can't be changed?

Some of the research I've done indicates that some individuals have fairly inflexible attentional styles. Typically these people describe themselves as being overloaded with stimuli most of the time—that is, they get confused because they can't deal with all the information coming in. The width of their attentional focus seems fixed and they are unable to broaden or narrow attention as the environmental situation changes.

What can you do to help these people?

Sometimes attentional width is fixed because individuals have a high level of trait anxiety—they are anxious most of the time, and this anxiety keeps their attentional focus narrow. For these individuals any procedure which lowers their level of trait anxiety results in their being able to broaden attention and to deal with more stimuli.

When your attentional width seems fixed and alterations in arousal level either do not help or are impossible, the best thing to do is to learn to be able to accept some limitations. If you are unable to modify your attention, the next best thing is to modify the environment so that it is not so confusing to you. For example, some sprinters wear dark glasses in order to reduce the number of distractions that might act to interfere with concentration. A coach or trainer can also be extremely helpful in reducing what a person must attend to by making sure that he does not try to get you to learn too many things at one time. He should stick to one or two major points and provide opportunities for you to repeat those to yourself. Actually there are many things that can be done. Basically they all involve providing more structure for you so that the number of possible choices you need to attend to are limited. Betty Perkins, an Olympic diving coach, accomplished this with some of her athletes by forcing eye contact and slowing the speech rate. She also moved closer to the divers to give instructions, resulting in less distractibility because the divers' visual fields were restricted.

If an athlete sees that he is getting confused, why doesn't he try these procedures on his own?

Let me begin by saying that some athletes do just that. Others, however, don't try to help themselves and I think that there are two major reasons for this. First, many athletes, because they are so competitive, do not want to

accept any limitations on their play and training procedures. They see limitations as things to overcome. This
means they challenge themselves rather than structure
their environment. They would rather fail over and over
again than simplify their environment and admit that they
have some limitations. Indeed they tend to see relying on
outside help in order to function better as the "coward's
way out," and this attitude is the single biggest reason for
athletes' inability to achieve their maximal level of performance.

Unfortunately the individual athlete's attitude in competitive situations is also often mirrored by his coaches,
fellow athletes, and parents. Many times these well-meaning people make it almost impossible for an individual to
accept the idea of personal limitation. Look to your own experience for examples. I am sure you have been in situations
where others exhorted you to "do better." Thus with the
personal and social pressures to be a winner, it's small
wonder that most of us have little tolerance for anything we
view as a weakness. Such ingrained responses are truly a
tragedy that can lead to chronic unhappiness—and it is far
more common than most of us realize. What it all boils
down to is that because we as human beings are unable to
accept some limitations, we never reach our full potential.
Instead we are continually frustrated by what we perceive
as personal failures. And our frustrations lead to more
arousal, and our performance is limited even more.

*You keep talking about lowering tension. Doesn't every-
one need some tension in their muscles to be able to function?*

Yes, of course we must have some muscle tension. The
trick is to discover just how much tension you need in order
to perform at your optimal level. The point I make is that
most of the time your tension levels are too high rather than
too low.

Does everyone have the same optimal tension level?

No. Everyone is built differently and everyone responds differently. Each of you must discover, through observation and experience, the optimal level of tension for yourself. This is not something that you can measure and then say, "Oh, I need *x* amount of tension in these muscles." Unfortunately measuring techniques, although they can be used to provide feedback about changes in tension levels, are hardly sophisticated enough to allow us to quantify the exact amount of tension you might need in a particular situation.

How do I find the optimal level of arousal for myself?

First of all, since we cannot use equipment to measure how much tension you should have, we must rely on your feelings and your ability to sense changes in your own level of tension. As soon as you learn (through feedback, autogenics, etc.) to become sensitive to changes in tension, it becomes a simple matter to notice how those changes affect your performance. By comparing your performance under conditions of varying tension, you can learn what your optimal tension level feels like. It's also important to point out that a tradeoff relationship exists that should be kept in mind.

Since both muscle tension and attention are affected by increases in arousal, it's conceivable that an increase in arousal might be helpful mentally because it would narrow attention and help you concentrate. At the same time, though, the increased muscle tension which might also result could be detrimental to performance. Thus it's important to keep *both* the physical and mental effects of arousal in mind when you're trying to determine what the optimal level of arousal is for you.

You mentioned earlier that one way of becoming aware of tension was to analyze the types of errors you make in competition. Well, how do I know that those errors are really due to tension increases and not just to some other problem such as stance, the wind, etc.?

This is a very important point. There are undoubtedly many times when you make mistakes which are not caused by tension increases. If you try to react to each and every one of these, you might be worse off than if you simply let them go.

The only way I can answer your question is to tell you to concentrate on looking for consistency in your mistakes. For example, the next time you throw a tennis ball too far out in front of you when serving, take some time to see if the wind is blowing or if you can detect tension in your neck and shoulder or if there are other signs of tension. Notice the playing conditions. Ask yourself if it is a particularly important point and has the same thing happened to you on other points like this one or in similar situations. If you find yourself answering yes to the questions, then tension is definitely increasing. If you're still in doubt, just hold your observations for a while and see if your problems continue.

How can I be sure that the procedures that you have presented in this book will help me?

The procedures contain no magic. The athlete must make use of the opportunity they provide to improve himself or herself. Knowing about the procedures is not enough—they must be practiced consistently to be of any use. The Fiberglas pole added a great deal to pole vaulting, but the athlete still has to learn to use and control the pole—the pole doesn't vault the athlete.

Now, speaking in theoretical terms, the procedures can help you in any or all of the following ways:

1. To raise or lower your tension level.
2. To broaden or narrow your attentional focus.
3. To teach you to passively concentrate.

4. To help you increase your self-confidence.
5. To relax.
6. To increase your endurance and reduce your sensitivity to pain.
7. To facilitate your memory, or ability to recall information.
8. To reduce fears.
9. To stop "choking."
10. To increase learning speed through improving concentration.
11. To systematically analyze your own behavior and that of your opponent in order to discover strengths and weaknesses.
12. To increase your motivation and enjoyment of the sport.
13. To increase your self-awareness.
14. To reduce the variability of your performance. To make you more consistent.

How good do I have to be at a sport before I can use these procedures?

There is no particular level of performance that you should have achieved. Anyone from a Little League player to a professional athlete can get something out of practicing these procedures. What you as an individual achieve will vary as a function of the level of your development.

Anyone can benefit from learning to relax. Relaxation results in your having more control over attentional processes, and it improves the consistency of your performance no matter what level of player you are. The use of these procedures to develop a passive concentration and then to apply that concentration to an athletic situation, as I've said repeatedly, is reserved for those situations where you have developed your skills to the level where no conscious thought is required. Likewise, the use of feedback procedures to increase your awareness of muscle tension in a sport only makes sense when you have already developed enough skill so that you can afford to direct your attention to other things, to making finer discriminations.

Again, for the procedures to work, you have to be willing to practice them. This usually requires a certain amount of dedication and motivation. For many athletes this motivation may not develop until they have already gained a fair amount of skill and have gotten some psychic rewards from their involvement in a particular sport. Thus it does seem highly likely that those individuals willing to invest in these procedures in a meaningful way will have already developed most of the basic skills required for their sport.

Won't practicing these procedures take away from my practice time?

This is a concern often expressed by your coaches, who are wondering how they can possibly squeeze one more thing into a tightly packed schedule. My experience, however, has been that the procedures do *not* take away from practice time.

To begin with, the actual learning of the relaxation procedures occurs away from the practice field. Through practice at home you soon learn to relax rapidly even while on the field—would you believe within thirty seconds? The rehearsal process is usually tied to the relaxation and goes on in earnest at home, though undoubtedly many athletes continue to rehearse at various times during practice. It's difficult to see how this would interfere with practice, except when the athletes are doing it at a time that they should be attending to something else. This problem, when it does occur, is not due to the rehearsal process but is simply a result of poor attentional control on the part of the athletes. And this is one of the problems which rehearsal can be used to overcome rather than accentuate.

Far from taking away from practice time these procedures usually enhance it. First, the relaxation results in more energy and more enjoyment—you are able to work hard and are more involved with the practice session. Secondly, the rehearsal process actually gets you practicing off the field as well as on it. Practice can become an around-the-clock thing if you find you can dig it! *Though I wouldn't recommend it*, I've had athletes so enthusiastic that they practiced relaxing between checkpoints while piloting their own planes!

Which of the procedures that have been presented would be best for me?

Once again, speaking in general terms, I can only give you some reasons for ruling out one or another procedure.

1. There are financial or time considerations, in which case the least expensive procedure is autogenic training, followed by meditation.
2. There is a negative attitude toward meditation and/or hypnosis. This is your privilege, but find out enough to make decisions based on knowledge, not myths.
3. Some athletes are unable to maintain the motivation to practice on their own. When this is true, the involvement of another person or the investment in some equipment (biofeedback) can often be helpful.
4. Occasionally athletes are interested in learning to relax only so that they can concentrate passively. When this is true, either meditation or autogenic training is the most direct procedure to use.
5. When the problem is a specific fear, such as being afraid of a ground ball, the procedure to choose is systematic desensitization.
6. If your arousal level is too low, some relaxation procedure used first and followed by imagery and rehearsal is appropriate.

7. On any occasion where new learning is to take place (e.g., reviewing game films, analyzing an opponent, learning new skills), use rehearsal and imagery procedures.

8. For awareness of changes in specific muscle groups, biofeedback is the treatment of choice.

9. For the reduction of pain which has already developed and for crisis intervention, hypnosis is perhaps the most useful procedure, with biofeedback running a close second—particularly when it comes to treating injuries.

10. To increase energy level, reduce fatigue, and improve your general attitude and feelings, *any of the procedures* can be used. Although the particular procedure that is employed can become an issue, by far the most important issue has to do with *how the procedure—* whatever it is—*is used.*

Aren't there some things for which everyone can use the procedures you have outlined—without having some problem to work on?

Yes, there are! I don't know of a single person who doesn't get anxious and upset from time to time. Nor do I know of any individual who is so perfect that there's no room for improvement. I think that a conscientiously applied program involving one of the relaxation procedures and the use of rehearsal techniques can be of benefit to everyone. The practice of these procedures insures that the individual would continue to grow and progress both in terms of gaining control over his own physiology and in terms of gaining understanding and insight into his own behavior—and that of others.

Is there a limit to my ability?

Yes, there is a limit to your ability, though I guarantee you will never reach it in all areas. I mentioned that most of us perform well below our potential, and in fact we are not even aware of what we are capable of doing. In spite of this, there are real physical limits which none of us can exceed.

How do I know if I am correctly practicing the procedures that you have outlined?

This is a very important question and not an easy one to answer. By far the best way to check this out is to sit down periodically with someone who has a thorough knowledge both of what you individually are trying to do and of the procedures themselves. When you don't have this kind of personal consultant service available—and this may well be the case—you are somewhat handicapped, but there certainly are some things you can do yourself to check up on your progress.

1. With the relaxation procedures (autogenics, progressive relaxation, and meditation), the major thing to watch for is that you don't try to force your attention on the mantra or on the feelings that you want to develop. This is self-defeating. Occasionally sit back and see how you are reacting to your own distractions. If you're learning to accept them passively and to then move on to other things, you're on the right track.

2. Check your progress daily over a couple of weeks. If you don't do this, you won't know if you are changing or not because you simply can't rely on your memory. If after a couple of weeks you are *not* feeling more relaxed, you're doing something wrong. Keep a diary of your feelings and responses to the practice. In this way you're more likely to pick up the small initial changes that tell you you're doing the right things.

3. Chances are that with biofeedback, systematic desen-

sitization, and hypnosis, you have someone available to work with you, so I won't comment specifically on these procedures.

4. When using rehearsal techniques to discover discriminate cues, there are a couple of things you should do to check your accuracy. First, once a cue is identified, see if your performance becomes worse when you don't use it. If it doesn't, then you really are not using the information the cue gives you, and it's not an important piece of information. Another way of checking the importance of the cue is to give it to a friend to use—tell him what to watch for, and see if the information helps. One of the things that you want to watch out for is engaging in too much rehearsal. Make sure that the rehearsal process occurs at times which do not interfere with actual competition. Finally, if you find that the rehearsal of errors is making you anxious, you should stop and get some professional advice.

If some athletes don't respond naturally to discriminative cues, then what is going on when a coach talks about a player with "great hands" or with "an instinct for the ball"?

A talented player reacts to information given off by the competitive situation. The rebounder in basketball knows by the way a shooter releases the ball (for example, how much spin it has, its trajectory, and the position on the court) where the ball is likely to end up if the shot is missed. He must be reacting to these cues because he certainly isn't reacting in the *absence* of any information. When a coach talks about instinct, he is often inferring that the talented athlete has some hereditary predisposition or ability to find the ball without any cues. As if by magic he appears where the ball is. Well, if the coach means that a talented athlete learns these things without formal training, then yes, there *are* athletes with an instinct for the ball. It is an instinct, however, that you and I can surely develop.

How do discriminative cues help? Do they actually make you faster?

If you think about it in terms of a race, they don't help you run any faster—they just help you get out of the starting blocks sooner, and your time is faster because you got a jump on the field. *Sports Illustrated* did an extended piece on Muhammad Ali in which they measured his ability to respond to a flash of light. What they found was that his response speed was just about average—no faster than for most of us. There are, however, a couple of major differences between most of us and Ali. First, once he initiates a movement, he completes it more quickly than we do. Second, he is able—and this is where the discriminative cues come in—to anticipate when his opponent is going to throw a punch. Thus, like a racer, he gets a quicker start.

Let me emphasize this point a little more because it really points out the importance of discovering the discriminative cues. Muhammad Ali at his prime could deliver a punch in only one-fourth of the time that it takes to begin to respond to a signal telling you to move. This means that if a boxer waited until Ali started the punch, there was no way he would ever block it. This indicates that a winning fighter must be able to identify the discriminative cues telling him that his opponent is going to throw a particular punch. He must anticipate the punch and begin to counter it even before an outside observer sees that the blow was coming. The boxer who ends up a loser often fails to learn what these cues are.

Aren't all the techniques that you have been talking about the very things that a good coach helps you do anyway?

I have known many coaches who do recognize—and respond to—many of the variables that I have talked about here. I certainly don't have any monopoly on how to relate to and train athletes. Unfortunately I think that it is becoming more difficult for a coach to do all the things we have talked about. There are only so many hours in the day, and a coach must play many roles. For that matter, I think that it is impossible for *any* individual to keep up with all the latest social, medical, educational, psychological, and physical developments in athletics. Look at George Alan with the Washington Redskins. He insists on working with older, more mature players who are already developed, and he has ten assistant coaches to help him out.

What can the coach do in order to improve or to function more effectively?

I can make some suggestions along these lines. However, I would not dare suggest that these be imposed on any particular individual. Let me respond, therefore, by pointing out what I think makes a good coach, and each of you decide whether or not you agree with me.

1. The coach should know himself. He should know the kinds of attentional errors *he* makes and how *he* responds under stress. This understanding of his own behavior is critical if he hopes to understand the different types of athletes he is working with. The good coach must know (recognize) his own strengths and weaknesses so that plans for games can be made with these in mind.

2. The good coach must be flexible and must be able to react to many different kinds of individuals. He must take the time to discover the discriminative cues that tell him how the athlete is reacting to what he is saying and that also allow him to anticipate the athlete's re-

sponse to his praise and discipline. He must be able to recognize the different attentional styles of the players, and he must have the interpersonal tools for adjusting his instructions to these styles.

3. He must have at least a conversational speaking knowledge of new techniques and developments in a variety of fields. He doesn't have to understand all the theory—but he should be aware of what exists. This knowledge is essential because the coach has to be able to recognize that at times there is a need to call in a consultant.

4. A good coach must be able to delegate responsibility to assistant coaches, consultants, and even the athletes themselves. If a coach cannot do this, he isn't able to take advantage of the expertise available to him; moreover, team morale goes down.

5. A good coach must take some chances and must allow himself and his athletes to make some mistakes. He must have the strength to be able to look at mistakes in an open way and learn from them.

6. A good coach must teach the athletes working with him to function independently—that is, he must teach them to assume responsibility for their own development and success.

As I think about what I'm saying, I realize that I am demanding that the coach be a very special person—a "man for all seasons."

What do you think are some of the most common mistakes in coaching?

There are several mistakes that I believe are fairly common. Most of them occur because the coach is inflexible and unable to adjust to different players and situations. These mistakes include:

1. The belief that all athletes need to be aroused. This causes some coaches to arouse players to the point of "choking."

2. The belief that all athletes must have a winning attitude. This is the philosophy that says, "Don't play for me unless you believe you can win." I suppose that ideally I would like to see everyone able to have that kind of confidence in themselves, but unfortunately many athletes don't have this kind of confidence. Moreover, very often it is not justified, and for a coach to insist that his players adopt that attitude under those conditions can cause more harm than good. The athlete who doesn't really believe he can win not only suffers the frustration and shame of losing but also ends up feeling as if he has failed the coach as well as himself.

3. The belief that all athletes on the team should think, look, and feel the same way. This is compounded by the belief that it's the coach's responsibility to treat them the same. Again, the coach must recognize that his athletes have individual needs and abilities. They all don't run or pass or tackle with the same ability nor do they all think or believe or feel in the same fashion. Rather than worrying about how individual team members feel if he treats them differently, the coach should work to have the athletes trust that whatever his responses are, they are honest and in the best interest of both the individual and the team.

I am convinced that socially we have reached a point where athletes now expect and even demand to be treated like individuals. This individuality is rapidly becoming a way of life, a philosophy, if you will. What this means is that the coach will get far, far more cooperation and respect by responding honestly to the individual than by treating everyone the same way.

Why is it that some people become so rigid that they coach or teach in only one way?

Perhaps the most obvious reason is that there is security in knowing exactly how you want to respond. Most of us have a tendency to stick with those things that have been successful for us in the past or with those procedures and techniques with which we are familiar.

It takes time to learn new methods, and they often don't work right away. In addition, if you are really involved with what you are doing as you learn a particular way of coaching, playing, or teaching, it begins to permeate your entire life. The coach who is really involved in his sport may look at the numbers 36-22-35 and think of a locker combination, of a particular signal in football, or of a win-tie-loss record. Most other people would think of a girl's measurements.

This total involvement on the part of a dedicated coach can narrow his perspective. He isn't up on many new techniques and procedures, particularly if they are peripheral to his field. He doesn't have the time or inclination to learn to talk to the athlete; he believes the athlete's job is to learn to talk to him. Under these conditions it is easy for a coach to fail to see that another individual is just as involved in the sport as he is.

I think that it all comes down to the fact that it is frightening to try something new. For this reason it's critical that a coach or an athlete be willing to take some chances. You don't learn anything new or improve what you do know without taking chances and making mistakes.

I would like to get back to the idea of arousing players. Don't pep talks work?

Yes, sometimes pep talks do work; many other times they fall flat. The coach can use the pep talk to arouse the players and get their adrenalin flowing, but it's critical that he also direct the athletes' attention towards positive thoughts. The danger with this kind of locker room arousal is that it can narrow attention. This narrowing means that it's imperative to focus on the proper stimuli and not on your own feelings of anger, frustration or fear.

I was talking to a reporter for *Sports Illustrated* and she told me that the late Vince Lombardi had a unique way of directing that narrowed attentional focus. Lombardi's players never lost a game—they may have been behind in the score at the end of a game, but they knew that if the game continued long enough, they would surely win. Thus they never lost, they simply ran out of time. If, like Lombardi, you can keep the players focused on believing in themselves and on playing the game rather than on worrying about running out of time or losing, then you can make successful use of the half-time talk.

How is it that when a young, inexperienced team competes against a better, more mature team, either they seem to play over their heads and win or they look terrible?

Assume for the moment that the attitude of the more experienced players is that "we know we're better than these guys. All we have to do is play our game and we'll win."

The members of the less experienced team are anxious, their arousal level is high, and their attention is narrowed. Because of their lack of experience these players have a tendency to be more affected by what is going on around them, and their performance will vary more than that of the more experienced players. What occurs very early in the game is very important to them. If they get a few lucky breaks, they focus on these positive experiences, catch fire, and play very well. Their enthusiasm and success then raise the anxiety level of the players on the other team and cause them to "choke." Given the time constraints of the game, the experienced team may just not recover.

In contrast, consider the situation in which the first

couple of breaks go against the younger team. With their high level of arousal and narrowed attention, it is easy for them to become trapped into focusing on these negative events. This results in further increases in anxiety and more deterioration in performance. They come unglued and lose by a wide margin.

This example, by the way, points out the fact that there is such a thing as a team high. On these occasions one or two individuals or a few lucky breaks can completely refocus the entire team's attention into a much more positive direction. Those players who are capable get their self-confidence back and those who doubt their own abilities become so excited by the way the game is going that they fail to think about themselves and play well. I think a great example of this was the 1973 Notre Dame–USC football game in which Anthony Davis ran the second-half kickoff back for a touchdown. A spark was ignited, and USC came from behind to crush the Irish.

From what you're saying, it seems as if it can be useful to arouse players sometimes. So who's right, the coach trying to psych the athlete up or the master of the martial arts trying to calm him down?

Actually, on occasion the coach may be right, but several important factors need to be considered before deciding to psych up an athlete.

1. What is the individual's arousal level to start with? He may already be so highly aroused that he can't attend to all of the things required for a good performance.
2. How complicated is the job he must perform? The more complex the task and situation, the *lower* the arousal level the athlete needs.
3. How important is fatigue—does the team need to conserve energy? If it's early in a long contest, you probably want to calm them down.
4. If you psych the team up, can you help them maintain

an appropriate attentional focus? Can you direct their attention to the task at hand, and can you ensure they will hang on to the belief that they will win? If not, increased arousal may hurt them.

5. How quickly does the individual recover from being aroused, and how rapidly does the competitive situation change? Individuals differ dramatically in terms of how long it takes them to recover—that is, to lower their arousal—from some stressful situation. If an individual does recover quickly and a short burst of energy is needed, arousal may be useful.

6. Does the coach want physiological arousal for strength or narrowed attention for concentration, or both? Relaxation and meditation procedures help individuals to learn to narrow and focus concentration without becoming aroused.

Once again I want to emphasize that the situations in which you would want to psych up an athlete are definitely very limited. There is too much psyching-up going on. You should treat arousal like a loaded gun. The athlete who is psyched up is bordering on being out of control. He has a limited control over his attentional processes, so he must rely more on his environment to provide direction. To function effectively, either he must be lucky or the environmental situation must be stable enough that he needn't fear having to make sudden or unforeseen adjustments.

Looking to the future, what do you see teams and individuals doing to better prepare themselves for competition?

You are already seeing athletes of all different levels of development reaching out to professional people outside their immediate area for assistance. The awareness of the importance of psychology and of the need to integrate mental and physical functioning is spreading, and I think that as more players make use of these procedures, the larger team organizations will find themselves being forced to hire professional consultants on a regular basis.

I think that Physical Education programs in colleges will start including courses in the psychology of athletics. Many colleges are already doing this. Before too long I expect such courses to be a required part of the curriculum for varsity athletes as well as for Physical Education majors. I think that emphasis will be placed on making these lab courses as well as theory courses because in this way the participants will actually learn to gain more control over themselves.

As a personal goal I hope at some point to be able to establish camps for athletes who want to learn to integrate their mental and physical functioning. The program, involving close cooperation between coaches, trainers, and psychologists, would be set up so that you spend two weeks at the camp. During the first three days you would undergo a comprehensive assessment procedure. This would involve psychological testing and a complete medical- and competitive-history interview as well as gathering information on your physical strength, speed, endurance, and quickness. This information would then be used by the staff to establish a training program tailored to your individual needs, and the remaining eleven days in camp would be spent in implementation of the program and would include a complete understanding of what is involved so that you could continue to progress at home.

How do I know if I need the help of a professional consultant? Can't I apply these procedures myself?

Of course, but there are limits to what you can do alone. Probably the best advice I can give you is to say that whenever you are in doubt about the way you are handling a situation, you should ask the professional advice of someone in whom you have confidence. This is particularly true if the problem involves learning how to lower your level of anxiety. This is important because your doubts about your progress are a source of anxiety that can doom you to failure. Often a quick "Yes, that's fine" from someone you trust is all that's required.

If you are continually redefining the problems that you want to work on—for example, you decide to rehearse a particular situation mentally, try it a couple of times without much success, and then decide that some other focus is better—then you should probably talk with a professional. Another signal is that you shift from procedure to procedure because you just can't seem to stick with one of them. You may try meditation for a while to learn to relax and then decide that it is not for you, so you try autogenics, and so on. If you find yourself vacillating between procedures, then get some professional advice.

There is one other situation to watch out for. Occasionally a problem is not what it appears to be. At first glance you attribute your anxiety to a game situation or to performance anxiety. However, as you begin to deal with that situation, you find that the problems are more involved and include complicated issues outside the athletic situation. When this happens, it's an excellent idea to call in a consultant.

How do I go about finding a consultant?

The best way is by what you have heard through others about the professionals in your area. Psychologists, like coaches, trade on their reputations. If you haven't heard of anyone in particular, there are a couple of other ways to go about finding names. Most libraries have a copy of the *National Register of Health Service Providers in Psychology,* published by the Council for the National Register of Health Service Providers in Psychology. This directory includes information on each psychologist who is a member of the association, including name and address, special areas of interest and work, dates of degrees, and institutions from which the psychologist graduated. A second source of information is the directory compiled by the Biofeedback Research Society. This group has a list of the names and addresses of those who are involved in the use of biofeedback in either research or private practice. For information write to Biofeedback Research Society, UCMC #202, 4200 East Ninth Avenue, Denver, Colorado 80220. A third source of information is a directory of those individuals using hypnosis in research and clinical practice. This directory is published by the International Society of Hypnosis, 205 West End Avenue, New York, New York 10023. A word of caution here: the fact that an individual's name is listed in any of these directories doesn't mean that he is necessarily appropriate to your needs nor does it mean that the respective societies (or I) recommend him.

How do I know if the psychologist I call can provide the service I need?

First, your chances are better if you call either a clinical, counseling, or consulting psychologist. Most psychologists will not charge you for providing information about their services—at least I don't know of any that do. If you have a particular problem or are seeking a particular kind of training (for example, biofeedback), say so. The psychologist in private practice is in the business of providing service. Don't be afraid to call and ask what services he has to offer and what his fees are.

What if everyone starts using these procedures?

I think that everyone *could* benefit from using the relaxation and rehearsal procedures—we would all be performing at higher levels. Even so, there will always be differences between individuals—and blessedly so.

Won't the types of analysis you describe take all the guesswork and excitement out of sports?

People have been analyzing horse races, the stock market, and roulette for years, and no one has come up with a system which takes all the fun out of the game. We can always improve our procedures and our ability to predict the outcome of games. Whatever we do, however, we will never be able to reach certainty. There are just too many things that can happen for us to be right all the time. When teams get too confident, they lose games they shouldn't. When we solve one set of problems, another set comes along to take its place. Far from taking the excitement out of sports, I think that these ideas and ways of analyzing situations should increase the excitement. The athlete will never run out of situations to analyze; he will never discover all the discriminative cues; and he will never be completely free of anxiety. The challenge is always the same one—to see how good you can become. The difference now is that we have another area—the mind—to use to our best advantage. Far from taking away from the excitement, we have created a new frontier for individuals to explore.

Notes

Chapter One
1. For more information on the history and practice of Karate see: Nishiyama and Brown, *Karate,* Tokyo, Charles E. Tuttle Co., 1959.
2. A complete description of Master Uyeshiba's revelatory experience is contained in: Uyeshiba, M., *Aikido,* Tokyo, Hozanshi Publishing Co., 1968.
3. Sargant, W., *Battle for the Mind,* New York, Doubleday, 1957.
4. For more information on this subject the reader is referred to: Pattie, F., "A Brief History of Hypnotism," in *Handbook of Clinical and Experimental Hypnosis,* Jessey Gordon (Ed.), New York, MacMillan, 1967.

Chapter Two
1. For more detailed information on attentional processes see: Nideffer, "Altered States of Awareness," in Wheeler, Deese, and Goodall, *Introductory Psychology,* Allyn and Bacon, 1975; Nideffer, "The Relationship of Attention and Anxiety to Performance," in *Coach and Athlete,* 1975.

Chapter Three
1. A good, though sophisticated review of literature on the subject is contained in: Easterbrook, J. A., "The Effect of Emotion on Cue Utilization and the Organization of Behavior," *Psychological Review,* Vol. 66 (3), 1959.
2. Thompson, R. F., *Foundations of Physiological Psychology,* New York, Harper & Row, 1967.

3. One of the physiological changes associated with increasing arousal is an increase in perspiration. As perspiration increases, it becomes easier to pass electric currents through the skin. By measuring the changes in an individual's skin conductance, it is possible to see changes in his arousal level.

4. Swimming performance as a function of the swimmer's arousal level:

400 M.R.	Low	Mean P	High
S.B.	1:01.8**	1:01.9*	1:02.2
D.G.	1:04.9**	1:06.8*	1:07.1
B.A.	56.0**	57.3*	57.3
M.R.	52.4**	53.8*	53.8
	3:55.1	3:59.8	4:00.4
1000FR			
J.T.	10:52.0**	10:52.0*	11:00.0
J.Tu.	11:39.7**	11:39.7*	11:58.8
200 FR			
R.H.	1:56.6	1:55.5*	1:55.5
J.E.	1:56.0**	1:57.8*	2:01.6
50 FR			
B.A.	22.8**	23.4	23.3
G.Y.	24.8**	24.8*	25.2
200 IM			
M.R.	2:13.6**	2:14.5*	2:17.3
S.B.	2:15.6**	2:16.5*	2:25.6
200 FL			
J.T.	2:16.5**	2:16.5*	2:31.8
S.I.	3:19.7**	3:23.1*	3:26.4

100 FR	Low	Mean P	H
B.A.	51.2**	51.5*	
J.E.	53.9**	53.9*	
200BA			
T.M.	2:14.9**	2:16.5*	2:
S.B.	2:21.7**	2:22.1*	2
500 FR			
J.T.	5:30.1	5:13.6*	5:
R.H.	5:19.0**	5:19.5*	5:
J.Tu.	5:20.7**	5:41.1	5:
200 BR			
D.G.	2:24.6**	2:28.0*	2:
A.D.	2:33.8**	2:36.6*	2:
400 FR			
M.R.	53.0**	53.7*	
B.A.	51.4**	51.7*	
J.E.	52.5**	53.8*	
R.H.	53.8	52.5	
	3:30.7	3:33.2	3:

**Indicates a time is equal to or lower than the same S's times at both higher arousal levels.

*Indicates a time is equal to or lower than the same S's times at the next highest arousal level.

Double Dual Meet Scores With Each Swimmer Competing Against Himself

R High   vs.   R Median
17   72

R Low   vs.   R Median
67   21

R Low   vs.   R High
77   10

Note: The mean change in time per subject per event, going from high to low arousal, is a minus 3 seconds.

Chapter Five
1. Correlations between the subjects' scores on the shortened form of the test with the full test (N = 25 Swimmers) are as follows: BET = .790, OET = .564, BIT = .921, OIT = .700, NAR = .668, RED = .686.

Chapter Six
1. Recommended readings: Marcues, F. L., *Hypnosis Fact and Fiction*, Baltimore, Penguin Books, 1959; Barber, T. X., *LSD, Marijuana, Yoga and Hypnosis*, Chicago, Aldine, 1970.

Chapter Seven
1. Schultz, J., and Luthe, W., *Autogenic Training*, New York, Grune and Stratton, 1959.
2. Wolpe, J., and Lazarus, A., *Behavior Therapy Techniques*, New York, Pergamon Press, 1966.
3. Vanek, M., and Cratty, B., *Psychology and the Superior Athlete*, Toronto, MacMillan, 1970.

Chapter Eight
1. Suggested reading: Tart, *Altered States of Consciousness*, New York, John Wiley and Sons, 1969.

Chapter Ten
1. For additional information see: Barber, T. X., DiCara, L. V., Kamiya, J., Miller, N. E., Shapiro, D., and Stoyva, J. (Eds.), *Biofeedback and Self-Control*, Chicago, Aldine, 1970, 1971, 1972, 1973.
2. Kamiya, J., "Conscious Control of Brain Waves," *Psychology Today*, *1*, 57, 60, 1968.
3. Budzynski, T., and Stoyva, J., "Biofeedback Techniques in Behavior Therapy and Autogenic Training." Unpublished manuscript, University of Colorado Medical Center, 1971.
4. A similar procedure is used to provide feedback about the presence of alpha waves. In this case electrodes are usually attached to the occipital and parietal areas of the brain. The presence of alpha is indicated by the appearance of a light or a tone.
5. Peppard, "Myotonic Muscle Distress: A Rationale for Therapy," *Athletic Training*, Vol. 8, 4, 1973.
6. Theta is a slow (four to seven cycles per second) brain-wave pattern found as individuals begin to become drowsy.

7. There are many equipment companies selling biofeedback devices. These are advertised in most copies of the *American Psychologist*, a monthly magazine published by the American Psychological Association, Washington, D.C.

8. Although most people have some alpha, there are exceptions. We have found people so alpha-dominant that even with sustained attention and with their eyes open, it is present. In contrast, there are other individuals who have no alpha at all, eyes open or eyes closed. Thus far we have not been able to identify reliable personality differences between these two groups.

Index

PLACE IN RETURN BOX to remove this checkout from your record.
TO AVOID FINES return on or before date due.

DATE DUE	DATE DUE	DATE DUE
0 6 6	0 9	————
AUG 2 5 1994 JUN 6 1995	————	————
0	JAN 0 8 2007 0 8 0 7	————
096 APR 2 1 1995	————	————
FEB 0 6 1996 R 4 1	————	————
1996 MAGIC 2	————	————
JAN 1 1 1999	————	————